Hertfordshire
COUNTY COUNCIL
Community Information

2 7 FEB 2010

10/12

Please renew/return this item by the last date shown.

So that your telephone call is charged at local rate,
please call the numbers as set out below:

	From Area codes 01923 or 020:	From the rest of Herts:
Renewals:	01923 471373	01438 737373
Enquiries:	01923 471333	01438 737333
Minicom:	01923 471599	01438 737599

L32   www.hertsdirect.org

D1438364

ROBIN HILDYARD

BROWNE MUGGS
ENGLISH BROWN STONEWARE

An exhibition of English Brown Stoneware
organised by the Ceramics Department, Victoria and Albert Museum,
September 11th – November 17th 1985

Published by the
Victoria and Albert Museum, 1985

Designed by
Grundy & Northedge Designers

Printed in Great Britain by
Jolly & Barber Limited

ISBN 0 948107 24 3

Front cover photograph
Tavern mug, made in London in the late 17th
Century (Catalogue No. 50).

Back cover photograph
Left to right. Jug, made at Bristol about 1825
(Cat. No. 212). Coffee pot, made at Eccleshill in
Yorkshire about 1840-50 (Cat. No. 357).
Basket, made at Brampton by S. & H. Briddon
about 1840-50 (Cat. No. 331). Puzzle jug, made
in the Brampton/Chesterfield area, dated
1802 (Cat. No. 293)

CONTENTS

PREFACE

Although examples of English brown stoneware are to be found in almost every Museum, collecting policies have resulted in either specialist collections of locally manufactured wares, or miscellaneous groups of pots with outstanding aesthetic or historic qualities. By building on a core consisting of the entire holdings of the Victoria & Albert Museum, with loans drawn from many Museums and several private collections, this exhibition sets out to show, for the first time, the full range of domestic stonewares made between c.1660 and the late 19th Century. While some dates and attributions are necessarily approximate, every effort has been made to include as many key pieces as possible. Attention is drawn in the catalogue to those regional characteristics which may assist with future identifications. Imperial dimensions have been given before metric, since these pots were frequently made to standard, inch sizes.

The staff of lending institutions and others, have given unqualified support. In particular, thanks are due to Judith Anderson, Derek Askey, Mavis Bimson, Hilary Bracegirdle, Lionel Burman, Rosemary Clarkson, Aileen Dawson, Dr. Graham Dawson, Richard de Peyer, Roy Edwards, Rosemary Ewles, Amanda Fielding, Eileen Gooder, Pat Halfpenny, Penelope Hatfield, Amanda Herries, Jonathan Horne, Margaret Hoskins, Tessa Murdoch, Jennifer Opie, Adrian Oswald, Elizabeth Owles, Julia Poole, David Roberts, Jessica Rutherford, Christine Smith, Karin Walton, Graham Wilkinson, Pamela Wood.

FOREWORD

Of all the utilitarian pottery made in England from the 17th Century, brown stoneware ranks as perhaps the least pretentious, and certainly the most durable. Yet, as with other common artefacts, the comparative scarcity of surviving examples belies the enormous scale of the industry that produced them, and the indispensable role that they played in daily life.

This exhibition owes much to the co-operation and generosity of many museums in the regions, in lending some of their best pieces to fill gaps and to provide back-up material for the Victoria & Albert Museum core collection. This book which thus encompasses a complete catalogue of the V&A holdings, launches the new *Ceramic Series*, which will cover both future exhibitions and guides to especially popular or rich areas of the outstanding ceramic collections.

Sir Roy Strong
Director,
Victoria and Albert Museum

THE NOTTINGHAM INDUSTRY

A Decantor

A Carved Teapot

A Capuchine

A Mogg

A Flower-Pot

A Carved Jug

Such as have Occation for these Sorts of Pots commonly called Stone-Ware, or for such as are of any other Shape not here Represented may be furnished w.th them by the Maker James Morley at y.e Pot-House in Nottingham

FIG. 1 *Proof for Morley's trade-card c.1700, in the Bodleian Library, Oxford.*

INTRODUCTION

B rown stoneware, a flint-like material impervious to water and immensely durable, was first made in Germany in the Middle ages and was exported in huge quantities to England, where it provided drinking vessels and containers for the tavern, kitchen and shop. As an apparently accidental discovery, the process of firing to about 1,200-1,400 degrees C. and throwing salt into the kiln where it vapourised and formed a coating of sodium alumina silicate over the vitrified pots and the kiln, remained a secret in England, despite the monopoly granted to Thomas Browne, Tobie Steward and Nicholas Burghley in 1614, and a patent issued by Charles I in 1626 to Thomas Rous and Abraham Cullen to make stone bottles. The high-temperature kiln patented in 1636 by David Ramsay, Michael Arnold and John Ayliffe perhaps brought stoneware production within reach, and certainly by the 1660s Simon Wooltus is said to have made *'Stone Gorges Muggs & Canns'* at Southampton, while his son Simon also made stoneware for a Mr Killigrew at Chelsea. A simultaneous, venture by immigrants from Germany or the Low Countries at Woolwich Ferry made stonewares for a local market, but failed to overcome severe firing difficulties.

The experiments of John Dwight at Wigan led to his first patent to make a variety of ceramic bodies, including *'Stone ware vulgarly called Cologne ware'* in 1672, the setting up of his pottery in Fulham and the subsequent spread of the technique throughout England. Dwight's fanatical pursuit after 1693 of those who infringed his patent has left us valuable evidence about his rivals and the early history of the industry, beginning with the Southwark pothouses of Matthew Garner & Luke Talbot at Gravel Lane and Moses Johnson at the Bear Garden, and John and David Elers who admitted making *'Browne Muggs'*, probably at their small Vauxhall pothouse. Counter-attacks by the Staffordshire potters Moses Middleton, Cornelius Hammersley and Joshua Astbury whom Dwight sued in 1697/8 imply that salt-glazing was already known there, while James Morley at Nottingham did not deny the accusation, and by about 1700 could offer in his advertisement (FIG. 1) a splendid array of pots. Moses Johnson, displaced from Southwark, took his skills to Bristol, where stoneware was made from about 1700.

After Dwight's death in 1703, the Fulham Pottery survived various vicissitudes without attempting to reproduce Dwight's finer wares, until the last descendant, Charles Edward White, died in 1859, leaving an unmodernised pottery shortly to be taken over by the enterprising Bailey, and after his bankruptcy in 1889, by the Cheavins (FIG. II). Several London delftware potteries added stoneware to their repertoire during the 18th Century, notably the Vauxhall Pottery (FIG. III), Griffiths & Morgan, and the Mortlake pottery of William Sanders. The fact that Gravel Lane also made delftware from the early 18th Century suggests that making only one type of pottery was uneconomical. By the beginning of the 19th Century, a small group of potters making exclusively stoneware were providing containers and drainpipes for an expanding London and Empire (FIG. IV). The Imperial Pottery of Stephen Green, later John Cliff, the London Pottery of James Stiff, the Lambeth Pottery of Doulton & Watts, and Thomas Smith, (FIG. V), began making and marking moulded wares, especially gin flasks, from the 1830s and 1840s, whilst smaller but productive potteries such as John Brayne, David Hill and the Bloodworths, have left no identifiable wares. Doulton emerged as the victor, finally absorbing his last rival James Stiff in 1913.

At Bristol, the few 18th Century stoneware wasters excavated in the city suggest that utilitarian wares were the main product, doubtless aimed at the export market. The magnificent sprigged hunting mugs made by John Harwell, probably at the Redcliff Back pottery of Thomas Frank, seem to have been exceptional pieces. More stoneware potters, such as Thomas Patience, James Alsop and John Hope, emerged as the delftware industry declined in the late 18th Century, and early in the following century John Hope and the Price and Powell families were concentrating on making bottles to complement those of the famous Bristol glass bottle industry (FIG. VI). The last pottery, Price, Powell & Co. was totally destroyed by bombing in the last War.

At Nottingham, small but highly skilled potteries grew up around the dominant Morley family, enjoying such a reputation that Nottingham Ware became the generic term for brown salt-glaze in the Midlands. Increasing competition from the cheap white stoneware of Staffordshire, together with the lack of local clay, led to a gradual decline in the second half of the 18th Century, despite the many new forms of decoration introduced by William Lockett and his followers. No pottery can definitely be attributed to Nottingham after 1800.

Crich in Derbyshire made wares indistinguishable from those of Nottingham, no doubt due to common clay sources and the family connections between the Morleys and the Dodds. Scattered potteries at Eastwood, Alfreton, Ilkeston, Belper, Bolsover and Chesterfield probably made mostly utilitarian wares until after the demise of Nottingham, when the tradition of lathe-turned lustrous domestic stonewares was developed and expanded until Derbyshire became the greatest producer during the 19th Century. In South Derbyshire, the Bourne famaily eventually owned Belper, Denby, Codnor Park and Shipley, while the potteries around Chesterfield were divided into those of Whittington, especially the Whittington Pottery of the Pearsons (FIG. VII), where bottles were chiefly made (FIG. VIII), and those of Brampton where a variety of moulded decorative wares were made by the Wright family at the Wheatbridge Pottery, the Briddons at the Walton Pottery, the Knowles at the

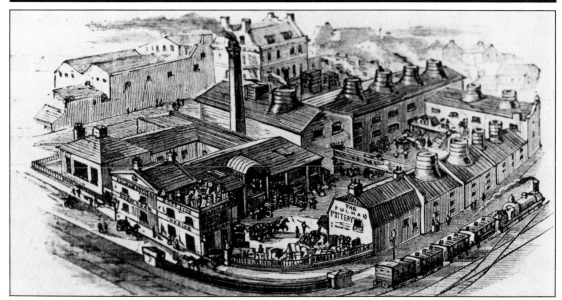

FIG. II *The Fulham Pottery, from Pottery Gazette 1882.*

FIG. III *The Vauxhall Pottery, drawn by Finlay in 1852.*

AT a Meeting, held this 16th March, 1795, of the Manufacturers of BROWN STONE WARE, in the Vicinity of *London*, and whose Names are hereunto subscribed, found it needful to make the following Regulations, and affixed the Price of STONE WARE; which, by Necessity of the Increase in the Use of the Articles used in the Manufacturing of that Ware, as well as the great Advance on the various Necessaries of Life, has induced us to adopt this Measure to make it publicly known.

	£	s.	d.			£	s.	d.	
½ Pint Stone Bottles and Jars	0	1	2	per Doz.	Pint Mugs and Gorges	0	1	9	per Doz.
¾ Pint Ditto .... Ditto	0	1	4	per Ditto	½ Pint . Ditto ... Ditto	0	1	4	per Ditto
1 Pint Ditto .... Ditto	0	1	9	per Ditto	¼ Pint . Ditto ... Ditto	0	1	2	per Ditto
1 Quart Ditto .. Ditto	0	2	6	per Ditto	Quart Spruce Beer Bottles ...	0	3	0	per Ditto
3 Pint Bottles, Jars, and Gorges	0	3	6	per Ditto	Pint ...... Ditto	0	2	0	per Ditto
2 Quart Ditto Ditto ... Ditto	0	4	6	per Ditto	Barrels	0	1	0	per Gall.
3 Quart Ditto Ditto ... Ditto	0	6	0	per Ditto	Liquid Blue Bottles, same as				
1 Gall. Ditto Ditto ... Ditto	0	8	0	per Ditto	Jars.				
6 Quart Ditto Ditto ... Ditto	0	12	0	per Ditto	Shop Pots	0	12	0	per Doz.
2 Gall. Ditto Ditto ... Ditto	0	16	0	per Ditto	And so on in Proportion.				
10 Quart Ditto Ditto ... Ditto	0	18	0	per Ditto	Printing, up to 1 Quart included, 4d.; including				
3 Gall. Ditto Ditto ... Ditto	1	4	0	per Ditto	1 Gallon, 6d.; all above, 1s.				
4 Gall. Ditto Ditto ... Ditto	1	12	0	per Ditto	Stone Pipes, 2s. each. Cistern Heads, 3s. each,				
5 Gall. Ditto Ditto ... Ditto	0	3	4	Each.	Offlets or Shoes, 1s. 6d. each. If exceeding the				
6 Gall. Ditto Ditto ... Ditto	0	4	0	Ditto	common Bore, to be paid for accordingly.				
Quart Mugs and Gorges	0	3	6	per Doz.					

To settle every Christmas and Midsummer, or 5 per Cent. for Money.

* The Prices to commence the 2d of April, 1795.

John Brayne. *James Pugh.*

William White. *Thomas Norris.*

George Moss. *Johanna Hemple.*

William Wagstaff. *James Ruel.*

Ann Jones. *Richard Waters.*

Welshpool & Payne Pottery, the Oldfields at The Pottery and Samuel Lowe at the Alma Pottery.

Tavern mugs were made by skilled potters in Staffordshire from about 1700, using the excellent local clays, but these were abandoned after experiments led to the white body with added Dorset ball clay and calcined flint. The impressive list of stoneware potters at Burslem in 1710-15, compiled by Josiah Wedgwood in 1765, included a minority of makers of *'Brown Stone'* and *'Freckled'* wares, suggesting that white stoneware may have taken over entirely by about 1720.

In Yorkshire, apart from Francis Place's attempts to make porcelain in ignorance of Dwight's patent, resulting in some delicate lathe-turned marbled stoneware cups and mugs which were probably made at Dinsdale in Co. Durham, no stoneware seems to have been made until the mid-18th Century. In the Bradford/Halifax area, the Wibsey Pottery made lustrous brown wares similar to those of Brampton, while the later Eccleshill Pottery, established with the aid of men and moulds from Staffordshire, made refined sprigged wares. Other Yorkshire potteries made only bottles throughout the 19th Century.

In Liverpool, by 1751 Dr Pococke noted that the Prescot potters made *'brown stone and work it, as they say, higher with the fire than at Lambeth'*. In 1770 and 1780 pothouses making *'Nottingham ware'* were advertised. In the 19th Century many potteries were active, although few seem to have left any marked wares.

The pottery established at Prestonpans about 1750 was followed by the Portobello Pottery in about 1770, both at first making white salt-glaze. Other potteries such as the Caledonian Pottery and Port-Dundas, made some decorated wares during the 19th Century, as well as the bottles which were the mainstay of the Scottish industry, centred around Glasgow.

For economic reasons, stoneware potteries sprung up wherever suitable clay and coal were present, mainly on the coal measures. London, dependent on imported materials, could compete with the mechanised industry of Derbyshire, where materials and labour were cheap and plentiful, by expanding rapidly, by making wares complementary to those of other centres and by exporting. Ready access to the export trade also ensured the survival of Bristol and Liverpool potteries. Fierce competition also compelled potters to develop and enlarge their kilns, which were being constantly eroded by salt vapour, and which might cause disastrous losses. Apart from the short-lived oval kiln at Woolwich, the earliest were based on the square delftware kiln, with single fire-box and arched roof with holes to act as flues. Dwight's kiln, eight feet square and which *'burnss extreame ferce'* with wood-firing, seems to have been generally copied in London, until the coal-fired bottle ovens of Staffordshire were adopted in the 18th Century; an early 18th Century example excavated at Hanley was 12ft. in diameter with 6 or 7 fire-boxes. At Nottingham, the square kiln seems to have been retained as being convenient for smaller potteries, for a drawing of a Nottingham

Ware kiln made by Josiah Wedgwood as late as 1779 shows a square kiln with five arches, which *'are taken down every oven full. The fire comes through the bottom of the kiln, and through the arches & the top of the kiln'*. Presumably such an up-draught kiln would give an oxydising firing and, apart from the severely limited capacity, might be difficult to control. Jewitt quotes Mr Goddard as saying that in 1820 the Lambeth kilns were *'seven or eight feet in diameter'*, but by 1878 some of the kilns of James Stiff were over 20 feet. Patents for improvements in kilns were taken out by Joseph Bourne in 1823 and 1847, by John Cliff in 1858, by William Northen in 1860 and by Henry Doulton in 1854 and 1867.

Saggars, called by Dwight *'Sluggs'*, were well known from delftware manufacture, and they were adopted immediately for the finer stonewares, having variously shaped holes to admit the salt vapour, and sometimes a slot to accommodate a mug handle. The more robust vessels, however, were stacked as tightly as possible and, like the German *'bellarmines'* show scars, dents, glaze drips and wide variations in colour, accidental effects of firing which were considered as necessary faults to be endured in the quest for efficiency, but which appeal to modern taste in the same way as *'raku'* fired pottery. Salt-vapour would not satisfactorily glaze the interior of bottles or jars, and William Powell even complained in 1832 that raw salt could sometimes become trapped inside bottles and contaminate the contents. From the 1820s, bottles which would be re-used were given an interior coating of lead-glaze to enable them to be properly cleaned. This problem was overcome by the invention of the liquid Bristol-glaze.

In an age when the craftsman potter is respected, it is important to remember the hazardous conditions in which stoneware was produced during the 18th and 19th Centuries, when forests of salt-glaze kilns were belching smoke and salt vapour into densely populated cities (FIG. IX). Even Dwight, whose ambitions to make porcelain produced some stonewares of extraordinary refinement, realised that mass-production was the only way to make the business viable, and his agreements with the Glass-sellers Company were deliberate attempts to supplant the imports from Germany by bottles of his own manufacture. The industry soon became the target of restrictive ligislation, first the crippling tax of 1695-8 to raise funds for the wars, the Act of 1700 whereby tavern mugs had to be stamped with an excise mark to certify the capacity, and finally the duty imposed during the period 1812-34 to protect the glass bottle industy.

Although no production figures exist for the earlier period, we know that the small Carlisle Pothouse in Lambeth in 1720 had two delftware and two stoneware kilns, while the inventory of the larger Gravel Lane pothouse in 1726/7 lists, amongst other stonewares, *1,006 stone mugs . . . . 570 lasts of flatt stone Jarrs & 9 gross of Falty do . . . . 6,156 pieces of stoneware . . . . 5 last of stoneware bottles and Jarrs, 60 lasts of handless bottles'*. Since a *'last'* is probably *'cast'*, the number of vessels with a total capacity of one gallon, the quantity is immense. By 1789, the growing industry at Chesterfield could boast three potteries employing 60 people, and in London, ten makers of brown stoneware signed a price agreement in 1795 (FIG. IV).

Upper Fore Street near the Three Merry Boys.

FIG. V *T. Smith's pottery in Lambeth, drawn by Finlay c. 1850.*

POWELL'S STONE-WARE POTTERY.

FIG. VI *Powell's pottery, Bristol, in the late 19th Century.*

More statistics exist for the 19th Century. Jewitt quotes Mr Goddard as saying that in Lambeth in 1820 there were *'6 or 7 potters, working some 16 small kilns'* and making bottles for beer, ginger beer, porter, cider, spruce beer and ink, pickle jars and hunting jugs, while at Codnor Park in 1828 Sir Richard Phillips reported that *'50 women and children finish 100 gross (of bottles) per day.... sell pints at 15d and 16d per dozen'*, and the number of Chesterfield potteries had risen to ten, employing 200 hands. In 1832 Joseph Bourne paid duty on 204 tons of bottles, equivalent to 456,960 pint bottles. Henry Doulton recalled in later years that Doulton & Watts in the 1830s employed 15 or 20 men exclusively for making Reform flasks, of which *'thousands'* were made. Brayley records in 1850 that the Vauxhall Pottery employed 60 men and boys, processed 800 tons of clay and 1,000 tons of coal per annum; Doulton & Watts had 100 persons, using 1,500 tons of coal and 1,000 tons of clay; Stephen Green employed 70 persons, and used 1,500 tons of clay, 100 loads of sand, 20 tons of flint and Cornwall stone, 12 tons of salt and 800 tons of coal, assisted by a steam engine. By 1860, Goddard stated that at Lambeth there were *'70 kilns turning out, perhaps, on an average £50. They consume upwards of 20,000 tons of coal. Twenty three thousand tons of clay are annually changed into useful articles, giving employment to more than 800 persons. The returns of the Lambeth potters cannot be estimated at less than £140,000'*. In 1878, James Stiff had 14 kilns on a two acre site, and a private dock beneath the Embankment, managing to survive in direct competition with Doultons until 1913.

Prices were always competitive, but can be misleading unless they are compared with other articles. Half pint Nottingham mugs cost 1¼d in 1720, and 1d in 1759, at a time when a Chinese porcelain cup in the same inventory was valued at 1/-, or twelve times as much. The pint version was 2d in 1759, rising to half-a-crown (12½P) per dozen in the 1770s. London pint mugs were cheaper at 1/9 (about 9P) per dozen in 1795, rising to 4/- (20P) by 1873, perhaps due to the inflationary effects of the Napoleonic Wars and the upheavals which followed it.

Throwers were quick and accurate. We cannot guess at the number of throwers who produced the average of 288 bottles per day per employee at Codnor Park in 1828, but at Price, Powell & Co. in the 1930s a good thrower could make 600 bottles, accurate enough to fit a mechanical filling machine. John Doulton could throw 200 two-gallon bottles per day in the early 19th Century. At Price, Powell & Co. a method of throwing the larger bottles inside wooden formers was being used in the 1930s.

In achieving the standardisation of the 19th Century, demonstrated by the wares shown in the 1795 London potters' price agreement, the founding of the London Potters' Association in 1853 and the identical range of wares offered by the Doulton & Watts and James Stiff catalogues in 1873, potters were guided entirely by commercial inter- ests. Whereas the white stoneware body of Staffordshire had been developed and refined to give creamware, blue transfer-printed ear- thenware and various stoneware bodies, such as those used for the popular smear-glazed stoneware jugs of the 19th Century, the areas into which a brown or grey body could expand were restricted to containers, domestic and electrical wares and sanitary goods. It was thus the tradition of lead-glazed slipware, still a village craft, which was picked up by the Arts and Crafts Movement and eventually incorporated into the Leach and Cardew schools of studio pottery. The inventive and technically brilliant pots of the Martin Brothers left no followers, while the Art Wares made by London potteries from c.1870 were based on German Renaissance stonewares, where colour and surface ornament were more important than form. Some artists exploited the plastic qualities of stoneware while others used it as a vehicle for interesting glazes, but the spontaneous qualities of once-fired, self-coloured brown stoneware are only now being re-discovered by a new generation of studio potters.

If the individual character of stoneware was finally sacrificed in the quest for efficiency, those pots made before the mid-19th Century show marked regional characteristics, caused by different clays being worked according to local traditions, often with different aims. The fine white body made by Dwight from dried and ground Dorset clay mixed with Isle of Wight sand soon gave way in London to the coarse sandy body, gritty and often underfired, which was given a dip of iron-bearing slip and sometimes, on decorated wares, an additional dip of white slip to lighten the lower half. The robust hunting mugs of Vauxhall and Factory 'B', as well as tavern mugs made at Fulham and elsewhere, sometimes had iron or manganese black detailing, further obscuring the sprigs. Improve-ments in kiln and clay led to the amber-coloured body with solid chocolate-coloured dip which became standard in the 19th Century, except for some light-bodied wares made by Stephen Green, William Northen and others. At Mortlake, the smooth creamy body and strong forms were ideally matched to the crisp sprigging. Bristol-glaze, at first imported from Bristol, was abandoned sometime after the mid-19th Century when the London potteries developed their own colourless version.

The recently discovered wares of Bristol have an almost white body with an even, freckled dip of coppery colour, turning in the late 18th Century to yellowish green or to the colour of black coffee. The sprigged decoration, supplemented by neat bands of rouletting, was extremely crisp and often highly idiosynchratic, matching the large, finely-potted mugs and harvest jugs peculiar to Bristol. Some completely grey wares, and others with grey interiors, suggest that reduction-firing may have been tried, or occurred by accident. Even the early 19th Century hunting mugs and jugs seem to have been lathe-turned, displaying the refine-ment that might be expected from a creamware-producing centre. The ovoid bottles and jugs are also distinctive. Bristol-glazing, invented by Anthony Amatt at Powell's in 1835, was soon generally adopted.

The burnished bronze colour of Nottingham lathe-turned stoneware has been attibuted to the use of ferruginous dips (in practice, thin red clay slip), but although the thin white line visible below the glaze may indicate a slip similar to that on Samian wares, where the mineral illite produced a natural gloss, there are no obvious signs of dipping. Given suitable iron-rich clay, heavy salting and the right firing cycle in a small kiln, such a colour might be produced naturally, as in Derbyshire, and certainly the different clays used at various times give wide variations in colour. Morley began to relieve the shiny surfaces of his pots by piercing

FIG. VII *Pearson's pottery, Whittington Moor (now demolished).*

FIG. VIII *Inspecting bottles at Pearson's, 1895.*

through double-walls, then incised *'snailshell'* and stylised foliage, often arranged in double bands. In the mid-18th Century William Locket added stamped decoration, incised flowers with rouletted shading and the use of sprigging. His followers added further variety, while applied bands of grog were used at this period to make *'breadcrumb'* decoration, and to make the coats of the Nottingham bears. The last quarter of the century brought incised decoration both coarse and fussy, as the industry declined.

Derbyshire pots appear to have been unambitious copies of Nottingham types with regional differences in the incised decoration, until sprigging and hunting jugs were quite suddenly introduced in the early 1820s, when also a greenish lead-glaze was first used to line pots. The Denby wares with their iron-specked body, reddish watery dip and sprigs outlined by a sharp tool are easy to distinguish, as are the lustrous brown coarse-bodied Brampton wares and the refined white-bodied wares with honey-coloured glaze, perfectly demonstrated in this exhibition by the two loving cups made for Jewitt in 1871. Jewitt mentioned one Brampton pottery using five local clays, for fire bars, bobs, and various strengths for placing in different parts of the kiln. Of all the surviving Derbyshire wares, the olive coloured bottles of South Derbyshire are by far the most numerous.

Staffordshire brown wares from the beginning were of very high quality, with a hard, white or grey body capable of being lathe-turned to extreme thinness, and dipped in lustrous brown slip. In their search for whiteness, the potters tried using engobes, later to be used on the cheaper kinds of white salt-glaze. The ear-shaped handles are typical of Staffordshire and Nottingham wares, and the almost identical types of rouletted decoration suggest close links. The period of production was too short for any development of shape or glaze to be noticable.

In Yorkshire, the local clays gave a dark brown colour, ideally suited to copying Derbyshire wares. At Wibsey, some pots were lined with white slip and lead-glaze of a duck-egg colour, while the Eccleshill Pottery from the mid-1830s made finely-potted wares with idiosynchratic sprigs, some of which derive from Staffordshire bone-chinas of the 1820s, while others seem to be versions of transfer prints. Some honey-coloured pots suggest that the high quality achieved by the pottery encouraged the importing of white clays.

So little is known of Liverpool stoneware, as yet, that it is not possible to point out regional features. Use of the sprig of boors, popular at Herculaneum, has resulted in the tentative attributions in this exhibition, but plain wares may have been almost all exported, as the number of early 19th Century spirit bottles with sharp-profiled necks and elegant lug-handled jars, some marked Yates and Swaine, found on the East Coat of America would suggest. 18th Century spirit bottles excavated at Cork seem to be of this type.

The markedly different stonewares of Scotland are rare in Southern England, in spite of the crisply sprigged wares of the early 19th Century, which might well have been exported, unlike the *'saut buckets'* and other pieces made for a local market. Some well-proportioned bean pots with bands of rouletting seem to have been made only in Scotland. The glaze and body is similar to that of Lambeth. Hunting jugs with moulded bodies are an unusual feature.

After the mid-19th Century, when interest in Britain's ceramic heritage was being stimulated by Solon, Jewitt and others, the discovery of the Dwight Heirlooms in 1860 focussed attention on so-called Fulham Ware. The main aspect of brown stoneware which appealed to the 19th and early 20th Century collector and connoisseur was quaintness, epitomised by the rustic London hunting mugs and the fine Nottingham loving cups with their homely inscriptions. The great collectors Willett, Greg, Glaisher, Franks and Lady Charlotte Schreiber gave good examples to the Brighton, Manchester, Fitzwilliam, British and South Kensington Museums, while the exclusively stoneware collection of Struan Robertson went also to Brighton. No attempts had been made systematically to collect the full range of products, since pieces were chosen for their decorative qualities or their inscriptions. That these represented the tip of the iceberg as far as stoneware was concerned is shown by the fact that the many tons of stoneware sherds excavated at Vauxhall have

FIG. IX *Lambeth waterfront c. 1860, showing Henry Doulton's drainpipe wharf and the long frontage of Stiff's pottery.*

yielded but one small fragment of a c.1720 hunting mug, which has enabled some 50 hunting mugs to be attributed. Commemorative pieces were fired with care and were handed down from generation to generation, as the engraved mounts of some show. By contrast, the mugs and bottles which formed the backbone of the industry were used to destruction and have almost all disappeared. It has, however, proved possible to construct typologies in some cases, for example from the four (of the five known) dated 18th Century bottles in this exhibition. Of the *'570 lasts of flatt stone Jarrs'* in the 1726/7 Gravel Lane inventory, and the many others known to have been made at Vauxhall and Fulham, only one of these delftware-type drug jars seems to have survived. No dated plain jars exist, although the forthcoming Reports of the excavations at Vauxhall and Fulham should give the date ranges of various types. Enough dated tavern mugs exist to show the changes in profile, and the change from the incised inscriptions of the first half of the 18th Century to the moulded names forming part of applied inn-signs during the 1750s, followed immediately by the use of printers' type. Many forms of domestic Nottingham stoneware are known only from excavation, and the Derbyshire wares were so ideal for their purpose that few changes were made over long periods of production, making dating very difficult.

It would now be difficult to assemble examples of English pottery as comprehensive as, say, the Lomax, Baring or Revelstoke collections of the period between the Wars. The mass of surviving 18th and 19th Century stoneware increasingly falls under the eye of the specialist collector or researcher, as new pieces turn up, old pieces from known collections are re-discovered and tavern mugs and bottles emerge from private excavations. Apart from the historical interest in a class of pottery that was once to be seen in every home, serving the same purpose as modern aluminium, enamelled steel, tin, stainless steel, plastic or moulded glass, the beauty of form which developed from the making of pots that were ideal for their function, with the minimum of time and materials, together with the random glaze effects on vessels which were never intended to out-live their immediate purpose and become art objects, can rival the more self-conscious decorated and commemorative wares, which still continue to demonstrate the skill and ingenuity of the stoneware potter, whose sympathy with his material could produce, under the name Brown Stoneware, such a diverse range of colours and forms.

1 BUST, probably JOHN DWIGHT

Grey overall, hand modelled.
FULHAM: c. 1673-5.   Ht. 7⅛ins (18.2cm)
Part of the heirlooms acquired by Thomas Baylis from Miss White, John Dwight's descendant, in 1861-2. Subsequently sold to C. W. Reynolds and dispersed at Christie, Manson & Woods in 1871.
Lit: Blacker 1922. Bimson 1961. Haselgrove & Murray 1979, frontispiece, pp 254-8. Oswald, Hildyard & Hughes 1982 pl. 1.
V&A Special Loan Exh. 1862, probably No. 3,693.
For discussion of the Dwight figures, see Bimson 1961. The reasons for identifying this bust as Dwight are explained by Haselgrove & Murray.
● V&A   Mus. No. 1053-1871

2 BUST, probably MRS. LYDIA DWIGHT

Grey overall, hand modelled.
FULHAM; c. 1673-5   Ht. 6⅞ins. (17.5cm)
Part of the Dwight Heirlooms: see Cat. No. 1.
Lit: Bimson 1961. Haselgrove & Murray 1979, pp 254-8.
V&A Special Loan Exh. 1862, probably No. 3,694.
This bust was called Mrs Pepys until Bimson (1961) recognised a family likeness. It is clearly a companion to John Dwight, Cat. No. 1.

Lent by the Trustees of the British Museum.   Mus. No. F7

3 FIGURE, LYDIA DWIGHT

Grey overall, hand modelled. The figure symbolically triumphing over death.
FULHAM; c. 1673-5   Ht. 11¼ins. (28.7cm)
Part of the Dwight Heirlooms: see Cat. No. 1
Lit: Bimson 1961. Haselgrove & Murray 1979 pp 254-8
V&A Special Loan Exh. 1862, No. 3,698
Lydia Dwight died in 1673.

● V&A   Mus. No. 1054-1871

4 FIGURE, LYDIA DWIGHT

Grey overall, hand modelled, the pillow collapsed in firing.
Inscribed on back: *Lydia Dwight dyed March 3 1673*
FULHAM; c. 1673   L. 9⅞ins. (25cm)
Part of the Dwight Heirlooms: see Cat. No. 1
Lit: Bimson 1961. Haselgrove & Murray 1979, pp 254-8.
V&A Special Loan Exh. 1862, No. 3,699

● V&A   Mus. No. 1055-1871

5 BUST, probably CHARLES II

Grey overall, hand modelled.
FULHAM; c. 1673-5   Ht. 7⅞ins. (20cm)
Part of the Dwight Heirlooms: see Cat. No. 1. Bought from funds of the
Bryan Bequest.
Lit: Rackham 1931. Bimson 1961. Haselgrove & Murray 1979, pp 254-8.
V&A Special Loan Exh. 1862, No. 3,692
Identified by Kingsley Adams of the NPG in 1951 as Charles II, after a Lely
portrait engraved by Blooteling in 1673.

● V&A   Mus. No. C. 52-1931

6 FIGURE OF NEPTUNE

Brown surface, made to imitate bronze.
FULHAM; c. 1673-5   Ht. 12¾ins. (32.5cm)
Part of the Dwight Heirlooms: see Cat. No. 1
Lit: Rackham & Read 1924 fig. 138. Bimson 1961. Haselgrove & Murray
1979 pp 254-8.
V&A Special Loan Exh. 1862, No. 3,711
Companion figures by the same modeller are Mars and Meleager (BM),
Jupiter (Liverpool Mus) and Saturn (destroyed Alexandra Palace 1873)

● V&A   Mus. No. C. 393-1920

7 FIGURES, ALLEGORICAL

Grey overall, hand modelled
FULHAM; c. 1673-5   Ht. 6⅛ins. (15.6cm)
Bought out of funds of the Bryan Bequest.
Lit: Rackham 1931. Bimson 1961.
These figures, not part of the Dwight Heirlooms, have been attributed to
Fulham on grounds of modelling similarities. The subjects have not been
identified, although C. 10-1931 is generally thought to be a Priest.

● V&A   Mus. Nos. C. 10, C. 11-1931

8 BOTTLE, "BELLARMINE"

Heavy greenish yellow glaze, misfired. Mask, and medallion of Stag's
Head.
FULHAM; c. 1675   Ht. 8¼ins. (21cm)
Given by Thomas Baylis to Lady Charlotte Schreiber in 1870.
Lit: Bimson 1961 p. 104, Haselgrove & Murray 1979 p. 260. Excavated at
the "walled up arched chamber" at Fulham in 1866: this was probably a
square-type kiln.

● V&A   Mus. No. SCH. II 57
This bottle may be seen in the adjacent Gallery 139.

9 BOTTLE, "BELLARMINE"

Dry grey/yellow glaze, misfired Mask, and medallion of CR and Fleur de Lys.
FULHAM; c. 1675   Ht. 8ins. (20.3cm)
Given to Lady Charlotte Schreiber by C.I.C. Bailey, the Fulham Pottery proprietor.
Lit: Bimson 1961 p.104, Haselgrove & Murray 1979 p.260,
Oswald Hildyard & Hughes 1982 pl.2.
Excavated at the "walled up arched chamber "at Fulham in 1866: this was probably a square-type kiln.

● V&A   Mus. No. SCH.II 56
This bottle may be seen in the adjacent Gallery 139.

10 BOTTLE

Freckled brown overall. Medallion of CR and Fleur de Lys.
FULHAM; c, 1675   Ht. 8⅜ins. (21.4cm)
Given by Lt Col K Dingwall DSO through the NA-CF.
Lit: Oswald, Hildyard & Hughes 1982 pl.2
Excavated in Holborn.

● V&A   Mus. No. C.590-1925

11 BOTTLE

Buff base, patchy freckled dip. Medallion of Cock and *W. MORRIS TEMPLE BAR*
FULHAM; c, 1675   Ht. 8ins. (20.3cm)
Mrs Sargeant Bequest.
Lit: Haselgrove & Murray 1979 pp 260-1. Oswald, Hildyard & Hughes pl.2
Other examples in Museum of London and Bimson Coll.

● V&A   Mus. No. 59-1967

12 BOTTLE

Shiny brown freckle with yellow streaks. Medallion of *R.C. 1675*
FULHAM; 1675   Ht. 7¼ins. (18.5cm)
Identical medallions excavated at Fulham Pottery: see Christophers, Haselgrove & Pearcey 1974 p.7 Fig. 5

Lent by the Museum of London

13 BOTTLE

Buff base, yellow/brown freckled dip with firing scars.
FULHAM; c. 1680   Ht. 8⅝ins. (22cm)
Dated by comparison with excavated pieces from datable deposits at
Fulham Pottery.

Private Collection

14 BOTTLE

Light greenish/brown freckle
FULHAM; c. 1685   Ht. 8⅜ins. (21.4cm)
Dated by comparison with excavated pieces from datable deposits at
Fulham Pottery.

Private Collection.

15 BOTTLE

Light freckle overall. Medallion with monogram JD.
FULHAM; c. 1675   Ht. 7⅞ins. (20cm)
Lit: Oswald, Hildyard & Hughes 1982 pl.4.
The initials JD almost certainly for John Dwight. A bottle of similar
shape with individual J and D medallions was also excavated: see
Christophers, Haselgrove & Pearcey 1974 p.9 Figs. 2, 3.

Lent by Museum of London and Fulham & Hammersmith Hist. Soc.

16 BOTTLE

Brown freckle overall, marbled with white and reddish black. Applied
initial C, and butterfly, hawks, heron and snail.
FULHAM; c. 1685   Ht. 6¾ins. (17.2cm)
Part of the Dwight Heirlooms: see Cat. No. 1. From the Harland Collection.
Lit: Bimson 1961, Haselgrove & Murray 1979 pp.256-7. Oswald, Hildyard
& Hughes Col. Pl.A.
Probably the "marbled porcellane" of Dwight's patent of 1684. Similar
examples at Fitzwilliam Museum and the British Museum. The initial C
may stand for Charles II; a bust of William & Mary applied to the
Fitzwilliam bottle indicates a date c. 1690.

● V&A   Mus. No. C. 101-1938

17 JAR

Buff, reddish brown freckled dip
FULHAM; late 17th Century.   Ht. 4¼ins. (11cm)
Formerly Tait Collection.
Lit: Oswald, Hildyard & Hughes pl. 22
Matches pieces excavated at Fulham Pottery.

Private Collection.

18 JAR WITH LUG HANDLES

Light grey/buff
FULHAM; late 17th Century.   Ht. 9ins. (22.8cm)
Excavated at Fulham Pottery. The shape perhaps copied from German
stonewares.

Lent by Museum of London and Fulham & Hammersmith Hist. Soc.

19 MUG, GLOBULAR

Grey, splashed with brown and blue oxide colours.
FULHAM; c. 1680   Ht. 4ins (10.2cm)
Given by J. H. FitzHenry.
Lit: Rackham & Read 1924 Fig. 141.
This type of lathe-turned mug may be dated by comparison with two
pieces in the Schreiber Collection, having mounts dated 1682.

● V&A   Mus. No. 896-1905

20 MUG, GLOBULAR

Lustrous brown dipped base, white top. Engraved with foliage and birds.
FULHAM; c. 1680-90.   Ht. 3¾ins. (9.4cm)
Formerly Franks Collection.
Lit: Blacker 1922 p. 62. Oswald, Hildyard & Hughes 1982 pl. 5.
The only known piece of wheel-engraved Fulham stoneware; perhaps
engraved in Bohemia.

Lent by the Trustees of the British Museum.   Mus. No. F 43

21 MUG, GLOBULAR

Light buff base, freckled patchy dip. Double walled, pierced by stylized flowers.
FULHAM; late 17th century.   Ht. 3⅞ins. (9.5cm)
Formerly Sheldon Collection, Glaisher Collection.
Lit: Rackham & Read 1924 Fig. 134, Rackham 1935 pl. 77A.
Exh. at Burlington Fine Arts Club 1914.
Presumably Dwight experimented with piercing before the technique was made popular by James Morley at Nottingham.

Lent by the Syndics of the Fitzwilliam Museum.   Mus. No. Gl. 1191

22 MUG, GLOBULAR

Patchy grey/buff overall.
FULHAM; late 17th Century.   Ht. 4⅝ins. (11.8cm)
Given by Mrs Hemming.
A waster, found near the site of the Fulham Pottery.

● V&A   C. 109-1923

23 MUG, GLOBULAR

Yellowish freckle overall. Medallion of a Turk's Head.
FULHAM; c. 1675.   Ht. 5¾ins. (14.6cm)
Lit: Oswald, Hildyard & Hughes 1982 pl. 3
A waster, excavated at the Fulham Pottery. Mugs with other medallions were found.

Lent by the Museum of London and the Fulham & Hammersmith Hist. Soc.

24 MUG, GLOBULAR

Patchy brown freckle overall. Medallion of CR and crowned rose.
FULHAM; c. 1675   Ht. 5¾ins. (14.5cm)
A bottle in Fulham Library bears the same medallion.

Lent by the Museum of London   Mus. No. A 11632

25 MUG FRAGMENT

Grey with manganese purple and cobalt blue. Applied floral medallion.
FULHAM; c. 1675
Excavated at the "walled up arched chamber" at Fulham in 1866, and
given to Lady Charlotte Schreiber. Many other fragments have since
been excavated, showing a wide range of coloured medallions, copied
from Westerwald prototypes or with Royal emblems.

● V&A   Mus. No. SCH.II 60.
This and the next entry may be seen in the adjacent Gallery 139.

26 MUG FRAGMENT

Grey with manganese purple and cobalt blue. Applied floral medallions.
FULHAM; c. 1675
See previous entry. This mug has been partially restored by adding
fitting fagments from recent excavations.

● V&A   Mus. No. SCH. II 59

27 Mug

Brown freckle overall. Lathe-turned with two bands of ribbing.
FULHAM; late 17th Century.   Ht. 7ins. (17.8cm)
Lit: Oswald, Hildyard & Hughes 1982 pl. 7.
This type has been excavated at Fulham. Since no examples with excise
marks are known, it probably ceased before 1700. Two other examples at
the Museum of London. Nominal quart capacity.

Lent by the Museum of London   Mus. No. A 23829

28 CAPUCHINE

Brown freckle overall.
FULHAM; c. 1690.   Ht. 4⅛ins. (10.5cm)
Lit: Oswald, Hildyard & Hughes 1982 pl. 6.
A waster excavated at the Fulham Pottery. Compare with the
Staffordshire capuchine in this exhibition. Pierced examples were
produced at Nottingham.

Lent by the Museum of London and Fulham & Hammershith Hist. Soc.

29 BOTTLE

Buff/grey base, freckled dip with yellowish pooling.
FULHAM; early 18th Century.   Ht. 8⅝ins. (22cm)
Lit: Oswald, Hildyard & Hughes 1982 Fig. 1, 3.
Matches fragmentary bottles excavated at Fulham Pottery, associated
with fragments of AR-marked mugs. Another example in the Mus. of
London.

Lent by the Museum of London.   Mus. No. A1119

30 MUG, WAISTED

Buff specky base, freckled dark dip. Conjoined WR excise mark
impressed below handle terminal.
FULHAM; early 18th Century.   Ht. 5ins.(12.8cm)
From the Guildhall Collection.
Waisted mugs also excavated at Vauxhall Pottery. The conjoined WR
excise typical of Fulham. Nominal pint capacity.

Lent by the Museum of London   Mus. No. 6450

31 MUG, WAISTED

White base, orange/brown dip, lead glaze.
Indistinct excise mark.
FULHAM; early 18th Century.   Ht. 5ins. (12.7cm)
Nominal pint capacity. Perhaps an example of the *Double-glaz'd Ware*
made at Fulham: see Daily Advertiser 15 June 1754, quoted by Nancy
Valpy,ECC Trans Vol. 11 Pt. 3 1983. Other pieces of this type are known.

Lent by the Trustees of the British Museum.   Mus. No. 1937-11-15-1

32 MUG

Grey base, light freckled dip. Applied inn-sign of horse.
Inscribed: Wm Wright at y^e Yorkshire Gray Hommerton.
WR excise mark.
FULHAM; second quarter 18th Century.   Ht. 5ins. (12.7cm)
Lit: Blacker 1922 p.48
Excise mark identical to examples excavated at Fulham Pottery.

Lent by Museum of London.   Mus. No. A24361

33 MUG

Grey base, light dip. Applied inn-sign of lion rampant.
Inscribed: *Ann Cleland 1748.* Conjoined WR excise mark.
FULHAM; 1748   Ht. 5⅛ins. (13cm)
Nominal pint capacity. Another similarly inscribed piece in Museum of
London, A4910, and fragments of two others (one excavated in
Pinsbury). Excise mark identical to examples excavated at Fulham
Pottery.

Lent by Museum of London   Mus. No. A4899

34 MUG

Grey specky base, tan freckled dip.
Inscribed: *Hump^y Warters at y^e Royall Oake Hawkurst Hyegate*
WR excise mark.
FULHAM; second quarter 18th Century.   Ht. 5ins. (12.8cm)
Nominal pint capacity. Excavated in Southwark, although Highgate is
near Hawkhurst in Kent. Excise mark, duplicated on a plain mug in Mus.
of London, B37, is identical to examples excavated at Fulham Pottery.

Lent by Museum of London   Mus. No. A11607

35 MUG

Buff base, dark dip.
Impressed: *Francis Smith Billericay 1794*
Conjoined WR excise mark, indistinct.
Probaly FULHAM; 1794.   Ht. 5⅛ins. (13cm)
From the Woolley Collection.
Lit: Rhoda Edwards 1973, No. 2/1.
Nominal pint capacity. Heavily potted. The excise mark and three-ring
foot are typical of Fulham.

Lent by the Minet Library

36 Mug

Buff base, dark solid dip.
Impressed: *I-Irish Yapton*
Conjoined WR excise mark, small and indistinct.
FULHAM; c. 1790   Ht. 6¾ins. (17cm)
Lit. Oswald, Hildyard & Hughes 1982 Fig. II, 9
Nominal quart capacity. The excise mark is identical to examples
excavated at the Fulham Pottery, while the three-ring foot is typical. The
exact dates of I.Irish, one of several at Yapton, cannot be established.

Private Collection

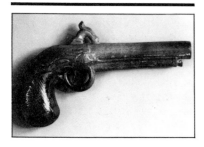

37 FLASK, PISTOL

Buff/lustrous brown
Mark, moulded: *Fulham Pottery*
FULHAM; c. 1840   L. 10ins. (25.5cm)
Another example, impressed *W Walker Windsor Berkshire 1842,*
Sotheby's West Sussex 15-18 Nov. 1983.

Private Collection

38 FLASK, CHRONOMETER

Impressed: *PATENT CHRONOMETER. E. HORNER, Grange Inn, Carey
Street, Lincolns Inn Fields.*
Impressed mark: *Fulham Pottery*
FULHAM; c. 1841-5   Ht. 5⅝ins. (14.3cm)
Dated from London Directories. Compare the Lady's Watch flask in BM,
and the marked T. Smith Railway Chronometer in the Minet Library, No.
14/6.

Lent by Museum of London.

39 HUNTING JUG

Cream base, patchy yellow/brown dip. Applied trees, topers, windmill,
hunt.
FULHAM; second quarter 19th Century.   Ht. 7ins. (17.7cm)
Formerly Tait Collection.
Fragments of all sprigs, including handle terminal, excavated at Fulham
Pottery.

● V&A   Mus. No. C. 68-1981

40 HUNTING JUG

Cream base, solid dark dip.
Applied trees, topers, shamrock/thistle/rose sprays, windmill, hunt.
FULHAM; second quarter 19th Century.   Ht. 6¼ins. (15.9cm)
Lit: Oswald, Hildyard & Hughes 1982 pl. 36.
Fragments of all sprigs, including handle terminal, excavated at Fulham
Pottery. Another example, impressed *HOT WATER PROOF,* in Minet
Library, No. 8/8.

Private Collection.

41 HUNTING JUG

Cream base, tan dip. Applied Trees, windmill, toper, church, hunt.
FULHAM (Bailey & Co.); 1874-89   Ht. 7½ins. (19cm)
An identical marked example, Oswald, Hildyard & Hughes 1982 pl. 37. A
loving cup with greyhound handles has been noted. The church sprig
seems to be peculiar to the Bailey period at Fulham.

Private Collection

42 HUNTING JUG

Buff base, reddish dip, frit lined. Applied windmill, topers, tree, hunt.
Impressed mark: *"THE POTTERY" FULHAM*
FULHAM (Cheavin period); c. 1900   Ht. 5½ins. (14cm)
The sprigs copied from Doulton.

Private Collection.

43 TOBY JUG

Lustrous light brown
Incised mark: *JC Fulham*
FULHAM (Cheavin period); late 19th Century.   Ht. 7¾ins. (19.6cm)
The JC monogram has been identified with James Caroll. At least one
piece with the JC monogram is marked *The Pottery Fulham*, indicating a
date after 1889.

● V&A   Mus. No. Circ. 651-1967

44 BOTTLE, "BELLARMINE"

Greenish grey/brown. Applied mask and medallion with stylised arms
and *GHTT.*
WOOLWICH; c. 1660-80   Ht. 6⅛ins. (15.5cm)
Lit: Pryor & Blockley 1978.
The short-lived kiln at Woolwich Ferry, active c. 1660-80, probably
preceded Dwight, and was probably begun by German immigrants. Few
Woolwich products have turned up elsewhere.

Lent by Plumstead Museum

45 MUG, GLOBULAR

Buff base, grey (misfired) dip. Applied medallion with stylised arms and
GHTT. Impressed circles on neck.
WOOLWICH; c. 1660-80.   Ht. 5⅝ins. (14.3cm)
Lit: Pryor & Blockley 1978.
See previous entry. One of many such wasters excavated at Woolwich.

Lent by Plumstead Museum.

46 MUG, GLOBULAR

Brown freckle overall. Medallion, moulded with *W E
BARRETT.-IN.-HANDYARD IN HOLBURN-LONDON-1668*
Possibly LONDON; 1668.   Ht. 5⅞ins. (15cm)
Although of German form, some German scholars have rejected this as a
Frechen product: the English inscription is unique, and the potting
unusually good. Simon Wooltus at Southampton and Mr Killigrew at
Chelsea were said to have made stoneware bottles before the Dwight
patent of 1672. For another example (possibly the same pot), see August
Demmin, *Keramik-Studien,* Leipzig, 1883, p. 64: then in the
Widerberg'sche Collection.

Lent by the Trustees of the British Museum   Mus. No. 1983-4-7-1

47 MEDALLION FRAGMENT

Dark and shiny freckle overall. For inscription, see previous entry.
Possibly LONDON; 1668.
It is not clear whether this medallion came from a globular mug or a
bottle.

Lent by the Museum of London   Mus. No. A 4903

48 COFFEE POT

Lustrous brown overall. Enamelled white and blue flowers.
perhaps LONDON (John Philip & David Elers); c. 1690-1700.
Ht. 5½ins (14cm)
Part of a group of "hausmaler" decorated stonewares, one dated 1706,
discussed by Rackham, 1942. The metalwork shape and use of
slip-casting, known to the Elers, suggest that this could be an Elers
product, after their stay in Staffordshire, where they made red
stonewares. David Elers, who learned the secret of salt-glazing at
Cologne, made *Browne Muggs & Red Thea potts* at Vauxhall from c. 1690
to the bankruptcy in 1700.

● V&A   Mus. No. C. 133-1938.

49 JUG WITH PINCH SPOUT

Buff base, dark freckled dip. Applied Arms of Norwich and initials
TB 1705
LONDON; 1705.   Ht. 8⅛ins. (20.5cm)
Lit: Tait 1970.
The initials may stand for Thomas Blofeld, a prominent citizen of
Norwich who stood as MP in 1705. This is the earliest dated London mug
with sprigged decoration.

Lent by the Trustees of the British Museum.   Mus. No. 1969-12-5-1

50 MUG

Grey base, freckled dip.
Mark or owner's initial: *W.*
LONDON; late 17th Century.   Ht. 5⅞ins. (14.8cm)
Given by A.L.B. Ashton.
Lit: Oswald, Hildyard & Hughes 1982 pl. 9.

● V&A   Mus. No. C. 174-1933

51 MUG, GLOBULAR

Grey base, freckled dip.
Inscribed: *Tho^S Foord at the Catts Lewis Sussex 1735*
WR excise mark.
LONDON (Southwark or Lambeth); 1735.   Ht. 7⅛ins. (18.1cm)
Formerly Willett Collection.
A late example of the globular tavern mug, which seems to have been
largely superseded by the cylindrical type in the early 18th Century.

Lent by Brighton Museum & Art Gallery

52 MUG

Grey base, freckled dip.
WR excise mark.
LONDON (Southwark or Lambeth); early 18th Century.
Ht. 6⅝ins. (16.8cm)
Lit: Askey 1981 p. 211. Oswald, Hildyard & Hughes 1982 pl. 10.
Nominal quart capacity. Thinly potted. A numeral 6 or 9 incised on the
interior base. Other mugs with identical excise marks in
Mus. of London.

Private Collection.

53 MUG

Grey overall, brown patches.
AR excise mark.
LONDON (Southwark or Lambeth); early 18th Century.
Ht. 3⅞ins. (9.8cm)
Transferred from Museum of Practical Geology, Jermyn Street.
Nominal half pint. A quart mug with identical excise mark, and two
bands of ribbing, in British Museum, Mus. No. F 29.

● V&A   Mus. No. 3750-1901

54 MUG

Grey base, dark dip.
WR excise mark.
LONDON (probably Southwark); early 18th Century.   Ht. 6¾ins. (17cm)
Formerly Guildhall Collection.
Nominal quart capacity. A waster with glazed fractures, excavated in
Southwark and presumably made there.

Lent by the Cuming Museum.

55 MUG

Buff specky base, matt dip.
Inscribed: *John Clifford att the Goate White Cross Street 1708*
AR excise mark.
LONDON (Southwark or Lambeth); 1708.   Ht. 5¼ins. (13.5cm)
The earliest dated London tavern mug. Nominal pint capacity.

Lent by the Museum of London   Mus. No. A4857

56 MUG

Grey base, freckled dip.
Inscribed: *Tho: parele (?)att y^e sum and punys in bishops gatt streett
1709*
AR excise mark.
LONDON (Southwark or Lambeth); 1709.   Ht. 5¼ins. (13.5cm)
From the Guildhall Collection.
Nominal pint capacity.

Lent by the Museum of London.   Mus. No. 6491.

57 MUG

Grey, iron-red rim and applied lion inn-sign.
Inscribed: *James Fidler in L . . . . . .th*
AR excise mark.
LONDON (Southwark or Lambeth); early 18th Century.
Ht. 7ins. (17.7cm)
Lit: Oswald, Hildyard & Hughes 1982 Col. Pl.B
Nominal quart capacity. The only known example of red colouring, as opposed to the iron-black splashes found on many sprigged mugs.

Private Collection.

58 PAIR OF MUGS

Buff base, dark freckled dip. Applied inn-sign of chained bull and cocked hat.
Inscribed: *Sam^{ll} Burchatt Lambeth* (one dated 1724)
WR excise, in oval.
LONDON (possibly Southwark, Gravel Lane); 1724.
Ht. 5¼ins. (12.8cm)
Given by Messrs Doultons, excavated on the site of the Doulton Pottery.
Lit: Oswald, Hildyard & Hughes 1982 pl. 11.
One Samuel Burchatt bore witness to the good character of Nathaniel Oade, the Gravel Lane pothouse proprietor, in 1718, which suggests that these could be Gravel Lane products.

● V&A   Mus. No. C.25, 26-1952.

59 MUG

Grey Base, freckled dip. Applied inn-sign of sugar loaf.
Inscribed: *Alex^{d} Peterson In King Harry Yard 1724*
WR excise mark.
LONDON (Southwark or Lambeth); 1724.   Ht. 6⅝ins. (16.8cm)
King Harry Yard is in Nightingale Lane, Limehouse. Around the handle is clipped a lead band, stamped WR, presumably to indicate that the capacity, a nominal quart, had been checked at a later date.

Lent by the Trustees of the British Museum.   Mus. No. F36

60 MUG

Grey base, reddish freckled dip.
WR excise mark.
LONDON; probably second quarter 18th Century. Ht. 6⅞ins. (7.5cm)
Miss Ethel Gurney Bequest.
The silver mount with unidentified maker's mark, and engraved 1=12=0,
perhaps a check on the capacity of a nominal quart.

● V&A   Mus. No. M.199-1939

61 MUG WITH PINCH SPOUT

Grey base, lustrous dark freckled dip, heavily salted.
Inscribed: Tho^S Tipp 1746
WR excise mark in oval.
LONDON (Southwark or Lambeth); 1746.   Ht. 6½ins. (16.5cm)
Nominal quart capacity.

Private Collection.

62 DOUBLE MUG

Grey base, light freckled dip. Medallions of a military officer.
Inscribed: Prosprous and Happy May they Be Who give Ben Brown their
Company 1748.
No excise mark.
LONDON; 1748   Ht. 4ins. (10.2cm)
From the Glaisher Collection
Lit: Rackham 1935.
Note the flaring foot, found on Factory "B" mugs of the same period.
Another London double mug is now in a Derbyshire collection,
impressed Thomas Genning Bury 1783.

Lent by the Syndics of the Fitzwilliam Museum.   Mus. No. Gl.1204.

63 JUG WITH PINCH SPOUT

Buff base, solid dark dip.
Impressed: RYE HOUSE HALL
LONDON; first half 19th Century.   Ht. 6⅞ins. (17.5cm)
Nominal quart capacity. Rye House, near Hoddesdon, gave its name to
the Rye House Plot in the late 17th Century. This pot may have been made
for the servants' hall. Quart "Measure Mugs" in the Stiff 1873 Catalogue
cost 5/6 (about 27P) per dozen.

Private Collection.

64 MUG

Buff base, solid dip.
Impressed: *VAUXHALL GARDENS*
LONDON; first half 19th Century.   Ht. 6⅝ins. (16.7cm)
Label on base: *A RELIC OF OLD VAUXHALL JULY 25 1859.*
Presumably acquired on the closure of the Spring Gardens.
A light stoneware mug in the Museum of London carries a sprigged view
of the Pavilion, similar to that found on transfer printed earthenwares.

Lent by the Museum of London   Mus. No. 63.37

65 BOTTLE

Buff base, highly freckled yellow/brown dip.
LONDON; early 18th Century.   Ht. 15ins. (38.2cm)
About two gallon capacity. The neck and body profile indicate an early
18th Century date. Comparable bottles, with squatter bodies, were
excavated at Vauxhall: see Roy Edwards 1984 pl. 47. Handle a
restoration.

Private Collection.

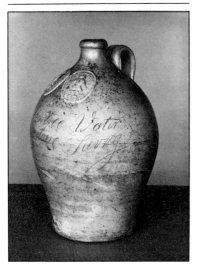

66 BOTTLE

Grey overall. Medallions of man on crutches, and man discarding
crutches, with *Drink and be Well.*
Inscribed: Iron Peartree Water near Godstone Surry.
LONDON; c. 1755.   Ht. 15⅜ins. (39cm)
Given by Major Dugdale.
Iron Pear Tree Water, a supposed cure for gout, was advertised in the
General Evening Post, 1752: bottles were sent to London, charged at 2/-
(10P) per gallon for the contents and a 2/- deposit on the two-gallon
bottle. The use of a moulded inscription in the medallion confirms a date
in the mid-1750s. Other examples at Brighton Museum, British Museum
and private collections.

● V&A   Mus. No. C. 467-1923

67 BOTTLE

Buff base, freckled dip.
LONDON (probably Southwark); late 17th Century.   Ht. 8⅝ins. (22cm)
Underfired stoneware, sandy body. For similar example, reconstructed
from fragments found on the South Bank, see Barton 1982, No. KB 52.
Other bottles of similar profile and body are in the Museum of London.

Private Collection.

68 BOTTLE

Freckle overall.
Inscribed: *John Price 1724*
LONDON (probably VAUXHALL POTTERY); 1724   Ht. 9ins. (22.8cm)
Lit: Oswald, Hildyard & Hughes 1982 pl. 19
Compare a similarly inscribed bottle waster excavated at Vauxhall,
Cockell 1974 pl. 138. Bottles inscribed *J. Price* and *Geo: Price* in the
Museum of London may be a little later, perhaps the 1730s-1740s.

Lent by Stoke on Trent Museum & Art Gallery   Museum No. 101 P52

69 BOTTLE

Grey base, finely freckled dip.
Inscribed: *Wingrave*
LONDON; c.1725   Ht. 8⅞ins. (22.5cm)
Compare the long, tapering neck with previous entry.

Private Collection

70 BOTTLE

Buff base, freckled dip
Inscribed: *Tho^S Rose 1739*
LONDON; 1739   Ht. 8½ins. (21.6cm)
Formerly Garner Collection.
Lit: Oswald, Hildyard & Hughes 1982 Fig. 1, 6.

Private Collection

71 BOTTLE

Grey base, freckled dip. Applied inn-sign of lion rampant.
Inscribed: *Edward Gallant*
LONDON; c. 1740   Ht. 8⅝ins. (22cm)
Exhibited *Fulham Pottery & Prints* 1929

Lent by Hammersmith & Fulham Archives Dept.

72 BOTTLE

Grey base, freckled reddish dip. Applied inn-sign of The Bull.
Inscribed: *Jnᵒ Fowler 1749*
LONDON; 1749   Ht. 7⅝ins. (19.3cm)
The blank area beneath the bull appears to have had a moulded name, erased when the inn-sign was re-used. This practice has been noted before. The large glaze drip on the front suggests that saggars were not used for bottles.

Private Collection.

73 BOTTLE

Grey base, freckled dip.
Inscribed: *T:S 1753*
LONDON; 1753   Ht. 9ins. (23cm)

Private Collection

74 BOTTLE

Grey base, freckled dip (much rubbed). Applied medallion, moulded with *Wᵐ: NASH. WOODS: CLOSE CHENEY: ALE MAN*
LONDON; c. 1755   Ht. 8½ins. (21.7cm)
From the Guildhall Collection.
Another example in Greg Collection, Manchester. Compare with a bottle at Colonial Williamsburg, the shaped medallion moulded with *Edward Atthawes 1755*. Edward Atthawes, a native of Mortlake, was witness to the will of William Sanders, the potter, who bequeathed money to Samuel Atthawes. There is a possibility that bottles of this type are products of the Sanders pottery at Mortlake.

Lent by the Cuming Museum

75 BOTTLE

Buff/brown base, heavy freckled dip. Applied inn-sign of the Three Crowns.
Impressed: *Iohn Lean Gravesend*
LONDON; c. 1764/8-1774   Ht. 8¼ins. (21cm)
Lit: Oswald, Hildyard & Hughes 1982 pl. 20.
The dates of John Lane's tenancy of the Three Crowns, 82-3 West Street, Gravesend, have been ascertained from the Rate Books and Publicans' Recognizance Book. The inn is now an amusement arcade.

Private Collection.

76 BOTTLE

Buff base, freckled dip.
Impressed: *Miland 12 Moore Street Soho*
LONDON; c. 1781-5   Ht. 7⅞ins. (20cm)
Lit: Askey 1981 p. 89

Private Collection.

77 BOTTLE

Buff freckled base, darker freckled dip
Impressed: Wm *Pater Oilman Hammersmith*
LONDON (possibly Fulham); c. 1820   Ht. 10ins. (25.5cm)
Lit: Oswald, Hildyard & Hughes Fig. 1, 9.
William Pater's business at King St. was close to the Fulham Pottery. A bottle of similar shape, impressed *Innel & Co. Long Acre,* datable to 1818, was excavated at the Fulham Pottery.

Lent by the Museum of London   Mus. No. 74.229

78 SPRUCE BEER BOTTLE

Light grey/buff overall
Impressed: *PAYNE'S Imperial White Spruce*
LONDON; c.1800   Ht. 6½ins (16.5cm)
Price Agreement of London Stoneware Potters in 1795 fixed price of quart spruces at 3/- (15P) per dozen. Doulton & Watts accounts 1819 list *Qt. Spruces.* Jewitt 1878 quotes a Mr Goddard, writing in 1860, "spruce-beer bottles (gone, with the beer, quite out of fashion) . . ." Surviving bottles are extremely rare.

Private Collection.

79 GOBLET

Cream base, freckled tan dip. Applied gridiron with *BEEF AND LIBERTY,* mitre and Prince of Wales Feathers.
LONDON (probably Mortlake, Kishere pottery); c. 1800
Ht. 8½ins. (21.6cm)
From the Willett Collection.
Lit: Blacker 1922 p. 108.
Presumably made for the Beefsteak Club in London. The glaze colour suggests the Kishere pottery, where a variety of sprigged giant goblets were made.

Lent by Brighton Museum & Art Gallery   Mus. No. Willett 575

80 BELLRINGERS' JUG, *GOTCH*

Grey base, freckled dip
Inscribed:
By Saml. Moss this Pitcher was given to the noble Society of Ringers at Hinderclay in Suffolk (viz) Tho. Sturgeon, Edwd. Lock John Hans Rich. Ruddocks Ra. Chapman. To which Society he once Belong'd 7 years and left in y One Thosand Seven Hundred & 2. From London I was sent As plainly does appear It was with this Intent To be fild with strong beer Pray remember the pitcher when empty.
On base:
25 March 1724
LONDON; 1724   Ht. 13¾ins. (35cm)
Lit: Howell 1978.
The date suggests that this was a New Year gift. Fragments of large jugs with ribbed necks have been excavated at Vauxhall, and were probably made by all the Southwark and Lambeth potteries, as well as Fulham.

Lent by the Hinderclay Parish Council

81 JUG

Brown freckled overall. Hand-modelled hops, corn, cornucopiae, caryatid merman supporting spout.
Moulded inscription: *James Sowerby 1781*
Mark: *R.B. de Carle fc* on handle. On base, *RPD*
LONDON (probably Lambeth); 1781   Ht. 8¾ins. (22.2cm)
Given by Mrs M.J. Miller.
Made for the botanist James Sowerby by Robert Brettingham de Carle, whose sister(?) Anne married Sowerby in 1786. de Carle, from a family of masons and sculptors at Norwich & Bury St Edmunds, was said to have

continued on next page

81 *continued*

worked at Mrs Coade's artificial stone factory at Lambeth; he exhibited
waxes in 1785 and died in 1791. For another jug made for the botanist
William Curtis, in Hants. Co. Museums, see Oswald, Hildyard & Hughes
1982 pl. 24. Another, inscribed *John Samuel Clack, born Jan. 16th 1781,* in
a private collection; see Connoisseur Vol. 3, 1902, p.269. The signature
RPD, possibly a thrower, has not been identified.

● V&A   Mus. No. C.90-1985

82 JUG

Buff base, freckled dip
Impressed: Wm Stone Walton 1792
WR excise mark, faint, in oval.
LONDON; 1792   Ht. 5¼ins. (13.3cm)
Another similarly inscribed, larger jug in Jonathan Horne Collection
suggests that a set of these may have existed. The excise marks indicate
that they are tavern measures.

Lent by Stoke on Trent Museum & Art Gallery   Mus. No. 302.P.35

83 DRUG JAR

Grey/buff freckle
LONDON; early 18th century.   Ht. 3¾ins. (9.5cm)
Formerly Tait Collection.
Lit: Oswald, Hildyard & Hughes 1982 pl. 22.
Fragments of stoneware drug pots, copied from delftware originals,
have been excavated at Vauxhall and Fulham, although this appears to
be the sole complete survivor. Probably the same as the *flatt stone Jarrs*
in the 1726/7 Gravel Lane inventory.

Private Collection.

84 PICKLE JAR

Grey, freckled dark dip. Applied inn-signs for the Four Swans, Grenadier,
Crown, King's Head (with *GR*), Duke of Marlborough (*DM*), Peal of Bells,
Sun, Jolly Sailor, Star, Hart, Noah's Ark, Bull, Griffin, Bell, Swan, Rose
(with *Wm Hasmere*), Castle, Angel, Spread Eagle, Angler.
Inscribed: *George Bennison & Sarah Nov 28 1752*
LONDON; 1752   Ht. 10¾ins. (27.3cm)
From the Glaisher Collection.
Lit: Rackham 1935, Oswald, Hildyard & Hughes 1982 pl. 23.

continued on next page

84 *continued*

No identical inn-signs have been discovered on tavern mugs, although this jar seems to represent the entire stock of one pottery. Note the partly erased name under the Rose.

Lent by the Syndics of the Fitzwilliam Museum   Mus. No. Gl. 1205.

85 JAR

Grey base, freckled reddish dip
LONDON; mid-18th Century   Ht. 10⅞ins. (27.4cm)
Lit: Oswald, Hildyard & Hughes 1982 pl. 22
Traces of paint adhering to body, indicating use as a Shop Pot.
Numerous fragments of this type of jar have been excavated at Fulham and Vauxhall.

Private Collection.

86 JAR

Matt buff base, freckled light dip. Lead-glaze lined.
Impressed: *R HORNE OIL & ITALIAN WAREHOUSE NEWINGTON CAUSEWAY*
LONDON; c. 1840   Ht. 6½ins. (16.5cm)
R Horne, dealer in oil and colour, and tallow chandler, was at this address from the 1830s. Exactly similar jars were salvaged from the wreck of the St. George, sunk off Jutland in 1811. The Price Agreement of 1795 priced pint jars at 1/9 (9P) per dozen.

Private Collection.

87 SHOP POT

Pinky buff base, solid brown dip. Applied Royal Arms and label.
LONDON; second quarter 19th Century.   Ht. 9⅞ins. (25.2cm)
Bears traces of paint on front. Later examples, such as those illustrated in Doulton & Watts and Stiff catalogues 1873 have rouletting. The pre-Victoria Arms continued in use long after 1837. Compare with Derbyshire examples in this exhibition.

Private Collection.

88 INK BOTTLE

Buff specky base, freckled dip.
Inscribed: *3* (probably for 3oz.)
LONDON; probably late 18th Century   Ht. 3¾ins. (9.5cm)
Another similar bottle in the Museum of London is impressed *4* on the
front: Mus. No. A5621.

Lent by the Museum of London   Mus. No. A25201

89 BOTTLE

Fine brown freckle overall.
Impressed: *J Cole*
LONDON; c. 1809-27   Ht. 4⅜ins. (11cm)
Lit: Askey 1981 p. 97.
Joseph Cole, colour and varnish maker, was listed at Leomond's-Pond,
Southwark, c. 1809-27, when Lowther became a partner. Compare
similar bottle in Museum of London, impressed *Berger & Sons.* (The
Berger paint firm were early customers of Doulton & Watts). Another
similar bottle in Museum of London impressed *HOWE.*

Private Collection

90 INK BOTTLE

Light buff/brown overall
Impressed: *SCOTT, 417 STRAND*
LONDON; c. 1830   Ht. 3¾ins. (9.5cm)
John Scott, Water Colourman to her Majesty, was at this address c.
1790-1839. The sharp shoulder profile suggests a date c. 1830. An
apparently earlier example also in the Museum of London.

Lent by the Museum of London   Mus. No. A10712

91 HOT WATER BOTTLE

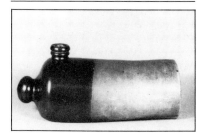

Freckled buff base, solid dark dip.
LONDON; c. 1830-40   L. 11⅞ins. (30.2cm)
Body thrown and flattened, a section being removed from the end.
Both glaze colour and neck form (compare Jim Crow flasks) suggest a
date c. 1830-40. Later hot water bottles had screw stoppers.

Private Collection

92 MONEY BOX

Patchy grey and brown freckle. Applied double frieze of foliage.
Probably LONDON; early 19th Century.   Ht. 4¼ins. (11.2cm)
Given by Mrs Radford.

● V&A   Mus. No. c. 31-1918

93 FLASK, TOBY PHILPOT

Buff base, dipped hat.
Impressed: *LAWRENCE & Co Cambridge.*
LONDON; mid-19th Century.   Ht. 6¾ins. (17cm)
Given by Lt. Col. K. Dingwall DSO through the NA-CF.
Members of the Lawrence family owned a wines & spirits business in
Bridge St. Cambridge in the mid-19th Century.

● V&A   Mus. No. C. 661-1920

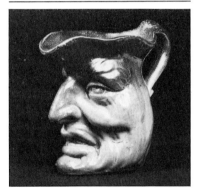

94 JUG, HEAD OF WELLINGTON

Buff base, freckled dark dip.
LONDON; c. 1830   Ht. 5⅝ins. (14.2cm)
The satyrical head of Wellington probably dates from his Administration
of 1829.

Private Collection

95 FLASK

Light brown/buff overall
Inscribed: *Bingley opposite Shore ditch Church*
LONDON; 1827-c. 1830   Ht. 7½ins. (19cm)
Benjamin Bingley moved to the King's Arms opposite Shorditch Church in
1827, and had left by 1831.

Lent by the Museum of London   Mus. No. C. 597

96 FLASK

Buff base, tan freckled dip.
Impressed: *PLOWMAN WINE AND SPIRIT MERCHANT 3 COMPASSES WANDSWORTH ROAD*
LAMBETH; c. 1840-50   Ht. 5¾ins. (14.5cm)
A waster excavated by Prof. Garner in the Lambeth/Vauxhall area. The Doulton & Watts accounts of 1819 list *Printing 50 Flat Bottles 6d.,* while the latest datable examples appear to be in the 1840s, when the moulded square types were introduced (see next entry). Plowman was at this address from c. 1840.

● V&A

97 FLASK

Buff base, solid dark dip.
Impressed: *J. BATTERSBY WINE & SPIRIT MERCHANT LEATHER MARKET TAVERN NEW WESTON ST BERMONDSEY. 3* (on base, for size)
LONDON; c. 1845-8   Ht. 6¾ins. (16cm)
Other similar flasks with publicans' names datable to c. 1840-50 suggest that the square type with fluted shoulder replaced the thrown *flat bottle* at that period. The type is shown in Doulton and Stiff 1873 catalogues, probably with Bristol glaze.

Private Collection.

98 FLASK, QUEEN VICTORIA

Buff/amber base, darker dip
Impressed: *W. EDWARDS Wardour St. Soho*
LONDON; c. 1837   Ht. 10ins. (25.3cm)
W. Edwards was landlord of the George, Wardour St. c. 1835-47. The moulded portrait based on a portrait by Sir George Hayter.

Lent by Brighton Art Gallery & Museum   Mus. No. 321057

99 FLASK, DUKE OF YORK

Buff base, shiny freckled dip
Impressed: *The Trade & Shipping Supplied. SAMUEL GARRETT Duke of York Wine & Spirit Vaults 29 High St Shadwell.*
Moulded: HRH DUKE OF YORK.
LONDON; c. 1832/5-8   Ht. 8ins. (20.3cm)

Lent by the Museum of London   Mus. No. A20865

100 FLASK

Light buff base, light brown upper parts
Moulded: *LEAGUE SUBSCRIPTION L250,000 R. COBDEN MP.*
LONDON; c. 1838-46   Ht. 12¾ins. (31.5cm)
The Anti-Corn Law League, formed by Cobden, Bright and others in 1838,
succeeded in having the Corn Laws repealed in 1846, after the Irish
potato famine of 1845.

Lent by Brighton Art Gallery & Museum   Mus. No. 321174

101 FLASK, THAMES TUNNEL

Buff base, patchy light dip
LONDON; c. 1843   Ht. 5½ins. (14cm)
Lit: Rackham 1935. Oswald, Hildyard & Hughes 1982 pl. 33.
From the Glaisher Collection.
Marc Brunel's Thames Tunnel was opened in 1843. The flask may have
been modelled after a contemporary engraving.

Lent by the Syndics of the Fitzwilliam Museum   Mus. No. Gl. 1217

102 JUG, SATYR HEAD

Brown base, solid dark dip
LONDON; c. 1840   Ht. 4ins. (10.2cm)
Several types are known, with or without spouts.

Private Collection.

103 SATYR CUP

Grey body, solid dip
Mark: monogram JR, IR, SR, FR(?)
probably LONDON; c. 1830   Ht. 4¾ins. (12cm)
Formerly Hill Collection.
A satyr cup, smaller and with mould differences, in the Minet Library,
No. 7/4, bears the same monogram. These two cups appear to have the
same characteristics as the next entry marked F*R.

Private Collection

104 SATYR CUP

Buff base, dark dip
Mark: *F*R* impressed
probably LONDON; c. 1830   Ht. 4⅛ins. (10.4cm)
The unidentified F*R may be a mould maker or a potter, and connected
with the maker of the previous entry.

Lent by Brighton Art Gallery & Museum   Mus. No. 321016

105 FLASK

Tan base, solid dark dip.
Moulded: *G. BROWNE OLD QUEEN ELIZABETH HEAD LOWER ROAD
ISLINGTON*
Mark: traces of inscription. . . . *11*
LAMBETH; (F. Wetherill); c. 1830   Ht. 8⅜ins. (21.2cm)
Derek Askey has noted that other flasks of this type bear faint
inscriptions: *Pub. by F. Wetherill July 27 1830 London.*

Lent by Brighton Art Gallery & Museum

106 JUG

Buff base, solid dip. Moulded with trophies and implements representing
various trades.
Moulded inscription: *Universal Nowlidge. The Union Jug.*
Mark: *Published According to Act of Parliament by F. Wetherill Modeler
No. 1 Cleaver Street Lambeth London*
LAMBETH (F. Wetherill); probably 1845   Ht. 9½ins. (24.2cm)
Probably made to commemorate the *National Association of United
Trades for the Protection of Labour,* established in 1845.

Lent by the Trustees of the British Museum   Mus. No. F 41.

107 FLASK, JIM CROW

Grey/buff base, dark dip.
Mark: *Pub^{ed} by F. Wetherill Novr 25 1836 25 Kennington Lane Lambeth*
LAMBETH; (F. Wetherill); c. 1836   Ht. 10½ins. (26.6cm)
Formerly Hill Collection.
Lit: Oswald, Hildyard & Hughes 1982 pl. 31.
Apparently the only surviving marked Wetherill flask of this type. The
model is taken from a music cover, and commemorates the visit of
Charles Dartmouth Rice to London in 1836, performing as Jim Crow.
Wetherill was both modeller and potter.

Private Collection

108 HUNTING JUG

Mat buff base, freckled dip. Applied topers, windmill, hunt.
Mark: *JAS CARROLL DEPTFORD POTTERIES ESE 1701*
LONDON (Deptford); c. 1900   Ht. 6⅜ins. (16.2cm)
The sprigs copied from Denby and Fulham, the terminal from T. Smith.
James Carroll took over the pottery from the Parry family c. 1891, when it was said to have been established for 190 years.

Private Collection

109 HUNTING MUG

Grey base, reddish dip. Applied trees, farms, figures, boxers/wrestlers, rosettes, hunt. Splashed with iron-black.
Inscribed: *Edw Slark 1727*
LONDON (Factory "B"); 1727   Ht. 8ins. (20.4cm)
Transferred from the Museum of Practical Geology, Jermyn Street.
A fox is sprigged on the inside bottom.

● V&A   Mus. No. 3689-1901

110 HUNTING MUG

Buff base, gritty dry dip. Applied plaques of sportsman, Royal Arms, Butcher's Arms.
Inscribed: *Thomas Dugard 1727.*
LONDON (Factory "B"); 1727   Ht. 7⅜ins. (18.7cm)
Lit: Blacker 1922 p. 58.
Exhibited *Fulham Pottery & Prints 1929.*
The inscription apparently cut through a layer of white slip, applied possibly to improve the appearance.

Lent by the Museum of London   Mus. No. A 5808

111 HUNTING MUG

Grey body, dark dip. Applied farms, trees, rosettes, hunt and central Punch Party.
Inscribed: *Richd Wheatland 1729*
LONDON (Factory "B"); 1729   Ht. 8ins. (20.5cm)
Formerly Lomax Collection.
Note that this Punch Party pre-dates Hogarth's painting of the Midnight Modern Conversation by two years, and cannot derive from it.

Private Collection

112 HUNTING MUG

Grey base, reddish freckled dip. Applied trees, rosettes, hunt, central plaque of The Forge. Splashes of iron-black.
Inscribed: $J^E S 1729$
LONDON (Factory "B"); 1729   Ht. 8¼ins. (21cm)
Given by J. Soria.

● V&A   C. 726-1923.

113 HUNTING MUG

Grey base, reddish dip. Applied trees, farms, hunt, central plaque of staghunt.
Inscribed: *Thos Watson 1736*
LONDON (Factory "B"); 1736   Ht. 8⅞ins. (22.5cm)
Formerly Gautier and Baring Collections.

Lent by Stoke on Trent Museum & Art Gallery   Museum No. 297 P35

114 HUNTING JUG

Buff/grey base, reddish freckled dip. Applied trees, farms, hunt, central plaque of stag hunt.
Inscribed: *Eliz Golding 1741*
LONDON (Factory "B"); 1741.   Ht. 12¼ins. (31cm)
Lit: Oswald, Hildyard & Hughes 1982 pl. 15.

Lent by the Museum of London

115 HUNTING MUG

Grey base, freckled dip. Applied trees, farms, hunt, central Punch Party.
Inscribed: *Francis Salt 1752*
LONDON (Factory "B"); 1752   Ht. 7⅞ins. (20cm)
Formerly Baring Collection.

Lent by Stoke on Trent Museum & Art Gallery   Museum No. 298 P35

116 HUNTING MUG

Grey base, reddish freckled dip. Applied trees, farms, inn-sign with *Wee: Three Loggerheads,* hunt, central plaque of Punch Party.
Impressed: *G. Jeffrey 1761*
LONDON (Factory "B"); 1761   Ht. 8⅛ins. (20.7cm)
Lit: Blacker 1922 p. 50
Lower half of body apparently dipped in white slip.

● V&A   Mus. No. SCH.11 63.
This may been seen in the adjacent Gallery 139.

117 HUNTING MUG

Grey base, dark freckled dip. Applied trees, farms, hunt, putti plaque, central punch party.
Impressed: *William Heath 1764*
LONDON (Factory "B"); 1764   Ht. 8⅞ins. (22.4cm)
Formerly Revelstoke, Baring and Tait Collections.
The central punch party is also found on a mug in Northampton Museum, impressed *Thomas Triplett 1761,* but has not been noted elsewhere. The putti plaque may have been moulded from a gilt base-metal snuff box of c. 1760.

Private Collection.

118 HUNTING MUG

Grey base, dark dip. Applied hunt, hand-modelled trees.
Inscribed: *John Rose Fill this with strong bear and wee will Fuddle our nose. 1713*
VAUXHALL POTTERY; 1713   Ht. 8⅝ins. (21.8cm)
Lit: Oswald, Hildyard & Hughes 1982 pl. 14.
The earliest dated Vauxhall mug. Undated mugs of similar type are in the Museum of London and Noel Hume Collections.

Private Collection.

119 HUNTING MUG FRAGMENT

Brown freckle overall. Part of hand-modelled tree.
Inscription: (On) Ba(nstead Downs a hare we found whi)ch Led (us all a-smoking round.)
VAUXHALL POTTERY; c.1720   Max. Width: 3¾ins. (9.5cm)
A waster with glazed fractures, excavated near the pottery site.
See Oswald, Hildyard & Hughes 1982 pp54-5.

Lent by Southwark and Lambeth Arch. Soc.

120 HUNTING MUG

Grey base, tan dip. Applied rosettes, trees, hunt, bust of Q.Anne.
Inscribed: *To the Pyouse Memory of Good Queen Ann. Tho^S Squier.*
WR excise mark.
VAUXHALL POTTERY; c.1720   Ht. 4⅞ins. (12.5cm)
Formerly Guildhall Collection.
Lit: Blacker 1922 p. 104.
Nominal pint capacity, the only known small Vauxhall hunting mug.

Lent by the Museum of London   Mus. No. 6435

121 HUNTING MUG

Grey base, brown dip. Applied hunt, central inn-sign of a fountain.
Inscribed: *William Gilbert 1720*
VAUXHALL POTTERY; 1720   Ht. 8ins. (20.3cm)

Private Collection.

122 HUNTING MUG

Grey base, freckled dip. Applied rosettes, bust of Q.Anne, hunt,
hand-modelled trees containing heads of Charles II.
Inscribed: *On Banstead Downs a hare was found which Led us all a
smoking Round. Abraham Harman att Lewis in Sussex 1724-5*
VAUXHALL POTTERY; 1725   Ht. 8⅜ins. (21.3cm)
Lit: Blacker 1922 p. 40.
The date 1724-5 suggests a New Year gift, ie, 25 March 1725.

Lent by the Trustees of the British Museum   Mus. No. F35

123 MUG

Grey base, freckled dip. Applied inn-signs of Charles I, Royal Arms with
CR, Prince & Princess of Wales, sedan chair, beefeaters, rosettes.
Inscribed: *God preserve King George and all the Royal Family Edward
Vaughan 1724*
VAUXHALL POTTERY; 1724   Ht. 8½ins. (21.6cm)

Lent by Brighton Museum & Art Gallery   Mus. No. 328024

124 HUNTING MUG

Grey base, reddish freckled dip. Applied inn-signs of Prince & Princess of Wales, beafeaters, trees, rosettes, hunt.
Inscribed: *Jn^O and Mary Finch 1726*
VAUXHALL POTTERY; 1726   Ht. 8¼ins. (21cm)

Private Collection.

125 HUNTING MUG

Grey base, freckled dip. Applied trees, rosettes, beafeaters, bust of Queen Anne, hunt. Splashed with iron-black.
Inscribed: *Wm Marsh. On Banse Downs a hair wee found thatt led uss all a Smoaking Round. 1729.*
VAUXHALL POTTERY; 1729   Ht. 9⅛ins. (23.1cm)
Lit: Blacker 1922 p. 46. Oswald, Hildyard & Hughes 1982 Col. Pl. C

● V&A   Mus. No. SCH.II 61.
This may be seen in the adjacent Gallery 139.

126 MUG, FRAGMENTARY

Grey base, freckled dip.
VAUXHALL POTTERY; c. 1715   Ht. 6½ins. (16.5cm)
Lit: Roy Edwards 1984.
Nominal quart capacity. Roy Edwards 1984 includes drawings of excise marks, both AR and WR, associated with this group.

Lent by Southwark & Lambeth Arch. Soc.

127 MUG

Grey base, freckled dip. Applied inn-sign of Queen's Head.
Inscribed: *Tho^S Scott*
WR excise mark.
VAUXHALL POTTERY; second quarter 18th Century.
Ht. 5¼ins. (13.2cm)
Lit: Cockell 1974, pl. 139.
Nominal pint capacity. The bottom has fallen out during firing.

Lent by the Cuming Museum.

128 BOTTLE

Grey base, freckled dip.
Probably VAUXHALL POTTERY; second quarter 18th Century.
Ht. 8⅛ins. (20.6cm)
Excavated by Prof. Garner in the area around the Vauxhall Pottery. The shape is similar to those excavated by Cockell and Edwards.

● V&A

129 PUZZLE GOBLET

Grey base, reddish freckled dip.
Inscribed: 1741
Probably VAUXHALL POTTERY; 1741   Ht. 3¼ins. (7.5cm)
Excavated by Prof. Garner in the area around the Vauxhall Pottery. The holes may have been only on the front. Too much is missing to be able to assess the original full height.

● V&A

130 BOTTLE

Dark brown overall
Impressed: *M. Martin Bridge House Vauxhall*
Probably VAUXHALL POTTERY; c.1816-28   Ht. 5ins. (13cm)
Lit: Oswald, Hildyard & Hughes 1982 pl. 29

Private Collection

131 BOTTLE

Buff base, reddish dip
VAUXHALL POTTERY; c.1840   Ht. 6⅝ins. (17cm)
Matches exactly fragments excavated at the Vauxhall Pottery. This seems to be the final form of the small globular bottle, ultimately derived from the German "bellarmine".

Private Collection

132 JAR AND LID

Light brown base, solid dark dip.
Impressed: *R.B. COOPER PATENTEE LONDON*
J.WISKER MANUFACTURER VAUXHALL
VAUXHALL POTTERY; c.1831-5   Ht. 8ins. (20.4cm)
Lit; Oswald, Hildyard & Hughes 1982 p. 52
R.B.Cooper's patent specification for ground lids and stoppers was
entered 1831, while Wisker entered a specification for improvements in
1833. This jar seems to have been made under licence from Cooper.
Another smaller version is known, 5⅛ins. (13cm) high, these two being
the only survivors. Neither jar has retained the brass(?) fittings for
securing the lids. For a glass decanter engraved *R.B.Cooper's Patent,* see
Christie's 22/11/83.

Private Collection.

133 FLASK

Buff/brown base, solid dip.
Impressed: *J.Cutbush 79 Blackman St. Borough.*
Mr. & Mrs. CAUDLE, Miss Prettyman, etc.
Mark: *DOULTON & WATTS LAMBETH POTTERY LONDON*
DOULTON & WATTS; c.1847-9   Ht. 5⅝ins. (14.2cm)
Joseph Cutbush was at the Star in Blackman St. c.1847-9. Compare with
the Stephen Green version in this exhibition.

Lent by Brighton Art Gallery & Museum   Mus. No. 321000

134 FLASK, LORD BROUGHAM

Cream base, tan dip
Impressed: *THE True Spirit of REFORM BROUGHAM, Reform CORDIAL*
Mark: *DOULTON & WATTS Lambeth Pottery 15 HIGH STREET LAMBETH*
DOULTON & WATTS; c.1832   Ht. 7⅛ins. (18cm)
Transferred from the Museum of Practical Geology, Jermyn Street.

● V&A   Mus. No. 3783-1901

135 JUG, HEAD OF NELSON

Light tan overall.
Mark: *DOULTON & WATTS LAMBETH POTTERY LONDON*
DOULTON & WATTS; c.1845   Ht. 7½ins. (19cm)
Lit: Oswald, Hildyard & Hughes 1982 pl. 44.
Probably based on the E.H.Bailey statue erected in Trafalgar Square in
1843. Made in several sizes. A grey Bristol-glazed version produced by
George Skey of Tamworth later in the 19th Century.

Private Collection.

136 JUG, BUST OF NELSON

Freckled tan overall
LAMBETH (possibly Doulton & Watts); c.1845   Ht. 11⅞ins. (30.2cm)
Transferred from the Museum of Practical Geology, Jermyn Street.
For a marked, more crisply moulded version, see Godden 1966 pl.245

● V&A   Mus. No. 3784-1901

137 SILENUS JUG

Buff base, dark dip.
LAMBETH (Doulton & Watts or S. Green); c. 1845   Ht. 7⅜ins. (18.7cm)
Mrs. D. B. Simpson Bequest.
The design adapted by Charles Meigh in 1844 from Poussin's *Bacchanalia*
in the National Gallery, and used by Staffordshire potters. Doulton &
Watts are known to have made *Bacchus Creams* in the 1840s, but for a
marked Stephen Green example, see Godden 1966, pl. 295.

● V&A   Mus. No. C. 31-1977

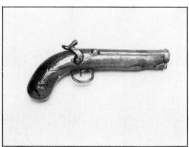

138 PISTOL FLASK

Tan overall.
Mark: *DOULTON & WATTS LAMBETH POTTERY LONDON*
DOULTON & WATTS; c. 1840   L. 10⅛ins. (25.6cm)
Given by Mrs Greig
The only dated pistol flask appears to be a Fulham example of 1842.
Compare the Fulham and Stephen Green versions in this exhibition.

● V&A   Mus. No. C. 915-1925

139 JUG

Buff base, tan dip, lined with white slip. Moulded with stag hunt and boar hunt.
Mark: *DOULTON & WATTS LAMBETH POTTERY LONDON*
DOULTON & WATTS; c. 1840
Lit: Oswald, Hildyard & Hughes 1982 pl. 43.
Produced in several sizes.

Private Collection.

140 BUTTER DISH & LID

Light brown body, dry brown lid. Moulded with vine leaf frieze, applied handles.
Mark: *Doulton & Watts 15 High St Lambeth*
DOULTON & WATTS; c. 1840   Ht. 5½ins. (14cm)
Lit: *The Doulton Story,* V&A 1979, No. B 12

Lent by the Museum of London   Mus. No. C 656

141 JUG

Buff base, solid dip.
Mark: DOULTON LAMBETH. Silver hall mark for 1869.
DOULTON; c. 1869   Ht. 6¾ins. (17.2cm)
Lit: Oswald, Hildyard & Hughes 1982 pl. 45
The mask with prominent bow on forehead seems peculiar to Doulton. Compare the T. Smith jug of similar shape. The Stiff version, termed *Pompeii,* was priced at 7/- (35P) per dozen for the ½ pint size in 1873.

Private Collection.

142 JUG

Buff base, dark solid dip.
Mark: *DOULTON LAMBETH* in oval
DOULTON; c. 1870   Ht. 6⅛ ins (15.5cm)
An identical *Antique* jug in the Stiff 1873 catalogue, priced at 7/- (35P) per dozen for the ½ pint size.

Private Collection.

143 FISH FLASK

Light brown overall
Impressed: *Brighton Fish. R. Cooper Railway Terminus Brighton*
Mark: *W Northen Potter Vauxhall Lambeth*
NORTHEN; c. 1840   L. 6⅝ins. (16.8cm)
For similar example, see Oswald, Hildyard & Hughes 1982 pl. 34.
For larger version, Godden 1966 pl. 446.

Lent by Brighton Museum & Art Gallery

144 BOOT FLASK

Pinky buff base, freckled dip.
Impressed: JONES Newington Butts (on sole)
possibly NORTHEN; c. 1840   Ht. 6ins. (15.2cm)
Jones was at the Waggon & Horses, Newington Butts, c. 1839-47.
A duplicate in Museum of London, as also a small barrel and a
Northen-type fish flask impressed *Jones Newington Rd,* all in a light
stoneware.

Lent by Brighton Museum & Art Gallery   Mus. No. 321079

145 POWDER FLASK

Buff body, freckled dip
Mark: *Smith Lambeth*
T.SMITH; c.1840   Ht. 7⅞ins. (20cm)
Smith seems only to have made pistol, powder flask and Ladies Watch
flasks. For a Stephen Green version, with slight differences in moulding,
see Godden 1974 pl. 75, and Oswald, Hildyard & Hughes 1982 pl. 38.

Private Collection.

146 JUG

Buff base, solid dark dip
Mark: *T.Smith & Co. OLD KENT Rd. LONDON* in oval
T.SMITH; c.1870   Ht. 9ins. (22.7cm)
Produced in several sizes, rarely marked. Compare the Doulton version.
This satyr mask is probably peculiar to Smith.

Lent by the Cuming Museum

147 HUNTING JUG

Matt buff base, tan dip. Applied windmill, topers, tree, hunt
Mark: *T.SMITH & Co. OLD KENT Rd.* in oval
T.SMITH; c.1880   Ht. 5¼ins. (13.5cm)
Lit: Oswald, Hildyard & Hughes 1982 pl. 48.
Two marked pint mugs with identical sprigs in Minet Library, Nos. 2/6, 2/7.

Private Collection

148 FLASK, Q.VICTORIA

Cream overall
Mark: *Published by S.Green Lambeth 20 July 1837.*
S.GREEN; c.1837   Ht. 11½ins. (29.2cm)
Given by Mrs Brownsword.
Exhibited *Queen Victoria* Exh. Tokyo 1979

● V&A   Mus. No. 497-1899

149 FLASK

Light buff/brown overall
Impressed: *Mr & Mrs Caudle. No! Mr Caudle I SHALL NOT GO TO SLEEP LIKE A GOOD SOUL. MISS PRETTIMAN* (on back)
Mark: *STEPHEN GREEN LAMBETH*
S.GREEN; c.1840   Ht. 6⅛ins. (15.5cm)
Compare the Doulton & Watts example.

Lent by the Museum of London   Mus. No. C.564

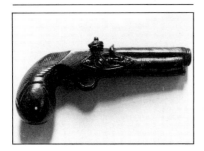

150 PISTOL FLASK

Dark brown overall.
Mark: *Stephen Green Lambeth*
S.GREEN; c.1840   L.8⅜ins. (21.2cm)

Lent by Brighton Museum & Art Gallery

151 FLASK, CHURCH DOOR

Buff base, dark dip
S.GREEN; c.1840   Ht. 10⅝ins. (27cm)
Marked examples exist.

Lent by the Museum of London   Mus. No. A13617

152 JUG, HEAD OF NAPOLEON

Pinky buff overall
Mark: *Stephen Green Lambeth,* in moulded cartouche
S.GREEN; c.1840-50.   Ht. 7ins. (17.7cm)
Transferred from the Museum of Practical Geology, Jermyn Street.
Produced in several sizes. Probably made during the 1840s when the
completion of Trafalgar Square stirred memories of the Napoleonic War.
A Wellington head jug by Stephen Green in Minet Library, No.7/12.

● V&A   Mus. No. 3782-1901

153 BARREL FLASK

Light buff overall
Impressed: *W Hammon Old Tom 1837*
Mark: *S Green Potter*
S. GREEN; 1837   Ht. 8¼ins. (21cm)
Produced in several sizes. This appears to be the only dated example.

Lent by Nottingham Castle Museum   Mus. No. 63. 311

154 TIPSTAFF FLASK

Dark solid base, light brown upper parts
Mark: *Stephen Green Imperial Potteries Lambeth*
S. GREEN; c.1840   Ht. 11¼ins. (28.5cm)
Other examples in the Museum of London, British Museum,
Brighton Museum.

Lent by the Museum of London   Mus. No. A 23221

155 JUG

Buff base, freckled dip. Moulded with heads of Victoria & Albert,
agricultural trophies etc.
Mark: *Stephen Green Lambeth,* in moulded cartouche
S. GREEN; c. 1840   Ht. 6¾ins. (17.2cm)
Made to commemorate the wedding of Victoria & Albert in 1840.
Other examples of various sizes in Brighton Museum, and Minet Library,
No. 7/1. The similarity of modelling between this and the *Union Jug*
suggests that F. Wetherill may have been responsible for the mould.
Lent by Brighton Museum & Art Gallery

156 MONEY BOX

Light brown base, solid dark dip.
Incised on base: *1874*
Probably J. STIFF; 1874   Ht. 4⅛ins. (10.5cm)
Lit: Rhoda Edwards 1973, No. 1/20
A Marked example, with *SAVINGS BANK* impressed over the doorway,
has been noted. Another Bristol-glazed example in the Minet Library.
No. 1/21
Lent by the Minet Library

157 HUNTING JUG

Light brown base, solid dip. Applied topers, trees, windmill, hunt.
Mark: *STIFF LONDON* in circle.
J. STIFF; late 19th Century.   Ht. 5⅜ins. (13.6cm)
The Stiff 1873 Catalogue lists 1 pint hunting jugs at 7/- (35P) per dozen.
Marked examples are unusual.
Private Collection.

158 BARREL, *BAR CASK*

Light brown, darker hoops. Applied Royal Arms of Q. Victoria.
Mark: *STIFF & SONS LONDON POTTERY LAMBETH* in oval. *2* (for two
gallon)
J. STIFF; c. 1880   Ht. 12¾ins. (32.5cm)
The Stiff 1873 Catalogue lists labelled 2 gallon spirit barrels at 3/8 (about
18P). Doulton versions often have vine leaf decoration and are more
elaborate.
Private Collection

159 TOBACCO JAR

Buff with tan hoops and pipe
Mark: illegible "diamond" mark and *GB* (?)
Probably J. STIFF; c. 1870   Ht. 4¾ins. (12cm)
Moulded in two halves. No design for this has been traced amongst Class
IV Registrations. The Stiff 1873 Catalogue lists ½ pint size at 1/2 (6P). For
a marked example, see Oswald, Hildyard & Hughes 1982 pl. 49.

Private Collection

160 SHAVING MUG

Buff base, lustrous dip. Applied windmill, topers, hunt.
J. STIFF; c. 1870   Ht. 5ins (12.8cm)
Typical Stiff sprigs, including the handle terminal.
The Stiff 1873 Catalogue lists *Figured Shaving Pots* at 7/- (35P) per
dozen.

Lent by the Museum of London   Mus. No. C. 573

161 HUNTING JUG

Cream base, freckled dip. Applied trees, hunt, central Punch Party.
MORTLAKE (probably Kishere); c. 1790-1800   Ht. 9¾ins. (24.8cm)
Formerly Tait Collection.

● V&A   Mus. No. C.64-1981

162 HUNTING JUG

Cream base, freckled dark dip. Applied trees, hunt, central plaque of
putti with lion.
MORTLAKE (probably Kishere); c. 1800   Ht. 6¾ins. (17.3cm)
Formerly Tait Collection
The putti plaque also occurs on squat hunting jugs of typical Kishere
type.

● V&A   Mus. No. C.66-1981

163 HUNTING JUG

Cream base, reddish freckled dip. Applied swags, topers, trees, hunt, central Punch Party.
Mark: silver mount hall marked for 1799.
MORTLAKE (probably Kishere); c. 1799.   Ht. 9½ins. (24cm)
Lit: Oswald, Hildyard & Hughes, 1982, Col.Pl.D

Private Collection

164 HUNTING MUG

Cream base, tan freckled dip. Applied trees, boors drinking, sportsman, hunt.
Mark: silver mount hall marked for 1798.
MORTLAKE (probably Kishere); c. 1798   Ht. 5⅛ins. (13cm)
Nominal pint capacity.

Private Collection

165 HUNTING MUG

Cream base, freckled dip. Applied trees, hunt, central Punch Party.
MORTLAKE (probably Kishere); c. 1800   Ht. 6⅞ins. (17.5cm)
Nominal quart capacity.

● V&A   Mus. No. 106-1878

166 LOVING CUP

Cream base, light brown freckled dip. Applied trees, hunt, central plaques of boors drinking and the Punch Party, flanked by classical figures.
MORTLAKE (probably Kishere); c. 1800   Ht. 8ins. (20.4cm)
Lit: Oswald, Hildyard & Hughes 1982 pl. 26.
Goblets and loving cups in many sizes exist, some plain, some sprigged, including the Kishere post windmill.

Private Collection

167 TOBACCO POT

Cream base, dark dip. Applied agricultural trophies, hunt, central toby
and plaque of boors drinking.
Mark: *Kishere Moatlake* (sic)
MORTLAKE (Kishere); c. 1800-10.   Ht. 5¼ins. (13.4cm)
Transferred from the Museum of Practical Geology, Jermyn Street.
Originally given by Dr. H. W. Diamond
Lit: Blacker 1922 p. 92. Godden 1966 pl. 331.
No Kishere pots of this type seem to have the domed lids found on pots
from other factories, but they may have been lost.

● V&A   Mus. No. 3771-1901

168 FLASK

Cream base, freckled dip. Applied Cupid Sleeping and Diomedes with
Palladion.
LONDON (probably Mortlake); c. 1800   Ht. 6ins. (15.3cm)
Thrown and flattened. The badly flaked sprigs and the rarity of sprigged
flasks might suggest that this was a stage between the flat thrown bottle
and the fully moulded types of the 1820s onwards. The Diomedes and
Palladion sprig derived from a Classical gem in the Chatsworth
Collection: see G. Lippold *Gemmen und Kameen,* Stuttgart 1922,
pl. XLII.

Private Collection.

169 JAR AND COVER

Dry, buff overall. Applied dancing putto musician, mother & child.
Impressed: *HENNERICH BARE*
Incised: *the 12 October 1800*
LONDON (probably Mortlake); 1800   Ht. 8¾ins. (21.4cm)
Given by Lt. Col. K. Dingwall DSO through the NA-CF.
Presumably made to commemorate a birth or christening. The dancing
putto appears on moulded jugs of Mortlake type, while the terraced foot
is not unlike some late 18thC Mortlake jugs.

● V&A   Mus. No. C. 654&A-1920

170 HUNTING JUG

Cream base, tan freckled dip. Moulded body with applied hunting
figures, dancing putto.
LONDON (probably MORTLAKE); c. 1800   Ht. 5½ins. (14cm)
Lit: Rhoda Edwards 1973 No. 8/6
Several sizes and types of these moulded jugs are known, mostly with
the dancing putto, and one with the dog & kennel on the next entry.

Lent by the Minet Library

171 HUNTING JUG

Cream base, tan freckled dip. Applied trees, windmill, gate, dog &
kennel, toby, hunt.
LONDON (probably Mortlake); c.1800   Ht. 8⅝ins. (22cm)
Formerly Tait Collection.
The dog & kennel sprig seems to tie this jug, and others with the tall
windmill, to the moulded baluster jugs (previous entry). Sprigs on this
group do not seem to appear on marked Kishere jugs, and it is possible
they may be products of Sanders' pottery.

Private Collection.

172 HUNTING JUG

Cream base, freckled dip. Applied trees, hunt, windmill, central Punch
Party flanked by classical figures.
Mark: *J*K* (for Joseph Kishere)
MORTLAKE (Kishere); c.1800-10.   Ht. 8⅝ins. (22cm)
Formerly Tait Collection.
An identical example in the Redstone Collection.

● V&A   Mus. No. C.63-1981

173 HUNTING JUG

Cream base, freckled dip. Applied hunt, central plaque of horses &
grooms.
MORTLAKE (Kishere); c.1800   Ht. 8ins. (20.5cm)
From the Glaisher Collection.
Lit: Rackham 1935.

Lent by the Syndics of the Fitzwilliam Museum   Mus. No. Gl.1209

174 HUNTING JUG

Grey base, tan freckled dip. Applied topers, trees, windmill, hunt,
central plaque of horses & grooms.
MORTLAKE (Kishere); c.1810.   Ht. 7ins. (17.8cm)
The blurred central plaque suggests that this squat jug is of later date
than the baluster example (previous entry) with crisper moulding.

Private Collection.

175 HUNTING JUG

Cream base, freckled dip. Applied trees, windmill, hunt, plaques of putti.
MORTLAKE (Kishere); c. 1810   Ht. 7⅞ins. (20cm)
The putto with hounds appears on a marked white stoneware goblet in
Mortlake Church. An identical jug in Museum of London.

Private Collection.

176 HUNTING MUG

Buff base, watery brown dip. Applied acorns, windmill, hunt, tree,
thatchers working on cottage.
Mark: *Kishere*
MORTLAKE (Kishere); c. 1820   Ht. 5⅝ins. (14.4cm)
Identical windmill on Mortlake-type hunting jug in Museum of London,
impressed *T & E BOYS 1820*

Lent by Museum of London   Mus. No. A27231

177 HUNTING JUG

Buff base, dark freckled dip. Applied with trees, *The Kill.*
Mark: *KISHERE MOATLAKE* (sic)
MORTLAKE (Kishere); c. 1810   Ht. 7ins. (17.8cm)
For similar example, see Blacker 1922 p. 120.

Lent by the Museum of London   Mus. No. A 28220

178 HUNTING JUG

Buff base, dark dip. Applied trees, topers, windmill, hunt.
Mark: *Kishere*
MORTLAKE (Kishere); c. 1810-20   Ht. 8⅝ins. (21.8cm)
Given by G. W. Ewen.

● V&A C. 137-1982

179 HUNTING JUG

Buff base, matt dark dip. Applied windmill, tobies, trees, hunt.
Mark: *KISHERE POTTERY MORTLAKE SURRY*[S]
MORTLAKE (Kishere); c. 1830-40
Given by Mrs Radford.
Lit: Godden 1966 pl. 331
A collander with identical sprigs and mark in the Redstone
Collection is dated 1842.

● V&A   Mus. No. C. 16-1923

180 HUNTING MUG

Light brown base, dark solid dip. Applied windmill, trees, topers, hunt.
MORTLAKE (Kishere); c. 1830-40   Ht. 6⅝ins. (16.8cm)
Formerly Hill Collection.
See previous entry for dating.

Private Collection.

181 JUG

Buff base, solid dark dip. Pinched face, incised details.
MORTLAKE (Kishere); c. 1820-30   Ht. 4¼ins. (10.8cm)
Set of five graduated jugs, marked *Kishere,* in Redstone Collection. A
large, elaborate example inscribed and dated 1822, was sold Christies
17/5/76 Lot. 90.

Private Collection

BROWNE MUGGS

BRISTOL & SOUTH WEST

182 LOVING CUP

Buff base, brown dip. Applied topers, putti, flower sprays, daisy border.
Mark: *H. CANNING WELLOW POTTERY HANTS*
WEST WELLOW (Canning); probably mid-19th Century.   Ht. 6¼ins.
(16cm)
Lit: Oswald, Hildyard & Hughes 1982 pl. 56
H. Canning seems not to have been included in local directories. No
other marked pieces are known.

Private Collection

183 HUNTING JUG

Buff base, freckled dip. Applied topers, trees, hunt, windmill.
Mark: *Crickmay Potter. . . . . mouth*
WEYMOUTH (Crickmay); second half 19th Century   Ht. 6⅜ins.
(16.2cm)
The windmill copied from Stiff. No potters of this name have been traced
in Weymouth, although a G. R. Crickmay was a well-known Dorset
architect of the 1880s.

Lent by the Trustees of the British Museum   Mus. No. 1912-10-2-4

184 JUG

Light brown base, dark dip.
Mark, incised: *No 1 Finest*
BRANKSEA POTTERY; mid-19th Century   Ht. 6⅛ins. (15.4cm)
Transferred from the Museum of Practical Geology, Jermyn Street.
Given by Col. Waugh, the proprietor of the Branksea Pottery, along with
a sample of clay. The pottery was still operating in the 1860s.

● V&A   Mus. No. 3726-1901

185 POSSET POT

Buff with reddish patches. Rouletted bands.
Probably BRISTOL; c. 1700   Ht. 6⅛ins. (15.6cm)
Formerly Gautier, Revelstoke and Baring Collections.
Lit: Oswald, Hildyard & Hughes 1982 pl. 51.
Exhibited *Fulham Pottery and Prints* 1929.
The very light colour, use of rouletting and similarity of the Nevers-type
handles to Bristol delftwares suggests a Bristol origin. The only known
stoneware posset pot of this shape.

● V&A   Mus. No. C.282-1976

186 MUG

Grey/cream base, freckled dip. Applied inn-sign of The Gun.
Impressed: *Tho^S Furner Brighelmstone 1766*
WR excise mark in oval.
Perhaps BRISTOL; 1766   Ht. 6¾ins. (17.2cm)
Excavated recently in Brighton. The stepped foot is not unlike fragments
in Bristol Museum, but quite untypical of London mugs. Note the archaic
use of *Brighelmstone* for Brighton: The Gun Inn (later Harrison's Hotel)
in Market Street was kept by a Mrs. Elizabeth Furner in 1800. Nominal
quart capacity.

Lent by Brighton Museum of Folk Life.

187 MUG WITH PINCH SPOUT

Grey base, freckled dip
Impressed: *T. WYATT 1767*
GR excise mark in oval.
BRISTOL; 1767.   Ht. 5⅛ins. (13cm)
Nominal pint capacity.
Purchased near Swindon. Other examples in private collections.
Compare next entry. The GR exise is identical to an example excavated
at Bristol and now in the V&A.

Lent by the Trustees of the British Museum   Mus. No. 1957-12-1-14

188 MUG

Buff base, dark dip.
Impressed: *T, Wyatt 1769*
WR excise mark, faintly impressed.
BRISTOL; 1769   Ht. 5½ins. (14cm)
Formerly Sheldon Collection. From the Glaisher Collection.
Lit: Rackham 1935.
The matt, almost black dip is consistent with Bristol stonewares, which
show wide variations in colour. Nominal pint capacity.

Lent by the Syndics of the Fitzwilliam Museum   Mus. No. Gl.1206.

189 BARREL

Grey middle, reddish patchy freckled dip.
Impressed: *Mary Brown 1794*
BRISTOL; 1794   Ht. (diameter) 6¼ins. (16cm)

Lent by Brighton Museum & Art Gallery

190 HARVEST BARREL

Cream body, yellow/orange dip.
Impressed: *Iohn: Evans 1797*
BRISTOL; 1797   Ht. 4⅛ins. (10.5cm)
A John Evans was apprenticed to John Hope, the Bristol stoneware
potter, in 1791, although several John Evans are listed in Directories.
Compare the W.Country slipware barrels, the Bristol delftware
examples and the creamware versions painted by Fifield.

Private Collection.

191 HARVEST BARREL

Dark brown overall.
Probably BRISTOL; late 18th Century   Ht. 4⅞ins. (12.4cm)
Given by Mrs Greig.
See previous entry. Several plain harvest barrels are in the Struan
Robertson Collection at Brighton Museum, which includes a high
proportion of Bristol pieces.

● V&A   Mus. No. C.909-1925

192 HUNTING MUG

Grey base, freckled dip. Applied coach & horses, trees, sun, birds, hunt.
Inscribed: *W^{C}M JH 1738*
BRISTOL (John Harwell); 1738   Ht. 9¾ins. (24.7cm)
Lit: Askey 1981 p. 45
The earliest recorded signed mug by John Harwell, who was
apprenticed to Joseph Taylor in 1733 and free in 1740, perhaps working
with his Master at the Redcliff Pottery of Thomas Frank. John Wedgwood
supplied him with earthernwares in 1761, 1767, 1768 at an address in
Rackhy Street, probably a 'Staffordshire Warehouse'. He died c. 1772-4.
For details, see R & P Jackson, 1982, pp 124-5.

Private Collection.

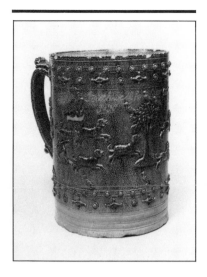

193 HUNTING MUG

Grey base, freckled dip. Applied hawks, trees with birds, sun, hunt.
Inscribed: *Southwell for Ever J H   W^{C}M 1739*
Mark on base: *John Harwell*
BRISTOL (John Harwell); 1739   Ht. 10ins. (25.6cm)
From the Schreiber Collection.
Lit: Blacker 1922 p. 36. Oswald, Hildyard & Hughes 1982 pl. 52.
See previous entry. Edward Southwell was the successful candidate in
the 1739 Bristol bye-election. Delftware bowls with the same inscription
may also be Harwell pieces, as he was a *gallypotmaker*. The recipients of
this mug and the previous entry have not been identified. Note that
Harwell became free in 1740: this might be an apprentice piece, made to
demonstrate his exceptional skill.

● V&A   Mus. No. SCH.II 62
This may be seen in the adjacent Gallery 139.

194 HUNTING MUG

Grey base, freckled dip. Applied cottages, trees, sun, hunt, central
Punch Party.
Impressed: *C Scott*
BRISTOL (John Harwell); c. 1760-70   Ht. 8¼ins. (21cm)
The sprig of plunging hound also on a large harvest jug at Colonial
Williamsburg, inscribed *The Floodland Jug my Frend will be if Master
Sam will Lend ye key. Mr Sam Pirkin;* other sprigs on this jug are common
to Factory "C", providing an overlap between the Harwell mugs and
Factory "C". For a large mug of the period between this and the 1738 and
1739 examples, see *Connoisseur* Jan. 1909: this was inscribed *John
Harwell 1754,* and is now lost.

Lent by Hammersmith & Fulham Archives Dept.

195 HUNTING MUG

Buff base, lustrous freckled dip. Applied trees, cottages, birds, sun, hunt.
Inscribed: *J. Harwell*
BRISTOL (John Harwell); c. 1760-70   Ht. 8ins. (20.3cm)
The blurred sprigs and glaze colour comparable with a two-handled mug inscribed *G.C. 1766* and a globular jug inscribed *G. Cotte 1766,* both made for George Cottey of Staple Fitzpaine.

Lent by Derby Museum

196 HUNTING MUG WITH PINCH SPOUT

Grey with light brown areas. Applied cottages, suns, hunt, central Nag's Head.
Impressed: *John Barnwell*
Incised: *1777*
BRISTOL: (probably Thomas Harwell); 1777.   Ht. 9¾ins. (25cm)
Lit: Oswald, Hildyard & Hughes 1982 pp92-4.
Thomas Harwell, son of John, became a free potter in 1774, being last recorded as a potter in 1788. The use of all the John Harwell sprigs after his death in c. 1772-4 suggests that this mug must be a product of Thomas. A similar piece in a private collection is impressed *C;Burges, Wallingford 1783.*

Private Collection.

197 HUNTING MUG

Grey base, matt dark dip. Applied trees, hunt, central stag hunt plaque.
Inscribed: *Robert Petch At Hermit-what Danby dale 1736*
FACTORY "C" (probably Bristol); 1736   Ht. 8ins (20.5cm)
From the Glaisher Collection.
Danby Dale is in Cleveland. The pot shows signs of slip-dipping to whiten the lower part.

Lent by the Syndics of the Fitzwilliam Museum   Mus. No. Gl.1200

198 HUNTING MUG

Cream base, freckled yellowish brown dip. Applied trees, rosettes, cottage, hunt, central stag hunt plaque.
FACTORY "C" (probably Bristol); c. 1735   Ht. 8½ins. (21.7cm)
Given by Mrs Greig.

● V&A   Mus. No. C.911-1925

199 HUNTING MUG

Grey base, freckled dip. Applied hunt, central panel of Punch Party, incised with Armourers' Company Arms.
Inscribed: *Tho^S Sparrow att Chippenham 1737*
FACTORY "C" (probably Bristol); 1737   Ht. 8¼ins. (21.5cm)
Lit: Charleston & Towner 1977, pl. 23

Private Collection

200 HUNTING JUG

Grey base, reddish freckled dip. Applied trees, cottages, rosettes, hunt, central inn-signs of Justice and Duke of Cumberland (moulded with *William Cumberland*).
Inscribed: *Wm Wright 1747*
FACTORY "C" (probably Bristol); 1747.   Ht. 12¼ins. (31cm)
From the Willett Collection.
The Duke of Cumberland was a national hero after his victory at Culloden over the Pretender, Charles Stuart, in 1746.

Lent by Brighton Museum & Art Gallery   Mus. No. 328122

201 HUNTING JUG

Buff base, freckled dip. Applied tree, cottages, hunt, central Punch Party.
Impressed: *Thomas Keys 1786*
Factory "C" (probably Bristol); 1786.   Ht. 8⅜ins. (21.3cm)
Private Collection.

202 BOTTLE

Freckled buff base, reddish dark dip.
Impressed: *1757 T Watts Fareham Hants*
BRISTOL; early 19th Century.   Ht. 15ins. (38.2cm)
About two gallon capacity. Note ovoid shape and high lip, common to
Bristol bottles. *1757* may be an identification number for the distribution
of spirits or cider. A bottle of similar shape, impressed *W MAPLES
SPALDING 1792,* in Spalding Gents Association.

Private Collection.

203 FLASK

Buff body, dark dip.
Impressed: *H. T. Evens Redcliff Hill BRISTOL*
BRISTOL; c. 1835.   Ht. 5¾ins. (14.5cm)
H. T. Evens, a retailer of wines and spirits, was recorded at this address
from the 1830s to c. 1855. Most Bristol stonewares after c. 1840 seem to
have been Bristol-glazed: this shape continued until the end of the 19th
Century, often marked *Price* or *Powell.*

Lent by Bristol Museum & Art Gallery

204 HUNTING JUG

Grey body, yellowish brown dip. Applied topers, watermill, windmill,
tree, haystack, cottage and agricultural implements.
BRISTOL; c. 1800   Ht. 10¾ins. (27.5cm)
Compare sprigs with next entry. Refined body and finely potted.

Private Collection.

205 PUZZLE JUG

Cream base, patchy tan/dark dip. Applied trees, topers, agricultural
implements. Handle with oak-leaf frieze.
BRISTOL; c. 1800.   Ht. 8⅞ins. (22.6cm)
Compare sprigs with previous entry. The only known puzzle jug, except
for the globular example impressed *JP 1828.*

Lent by Jonathan Horne

206 HUNTING JUG

Cream base, yellow/reddish dip. Applied rose bush, tree, Bacchanalian putti, hunt.
BRISTOL; c. 1800.   Ht. 9ins. (22.9cm)
Formerly Tait Collection.
Compare the sprigs with Bright Goblet. These seem peculiar to Bristol stonewares.

● V&A   Mus. No. C. 67-1981

207 HUNTING JUG

Buff base, dark freckled dip. Applied windmill, trees, topers, hunt, handle terminal with leaf and Prince of Wales feathers.
BRISTOL; early 19th Century   Ht. 6½ins. (16.5cm)
Note the ovoid body.

Private Collection.

208 HUNTING JUG

Cream base, yellowish reddish dip. Applied trees, fruit basket, topers, hunt.
BRISTOL; early 19th Century   Ht. 5ins. (12.7cm)
Mrs D. B. Simpson Bequest.
The base dipped in white slip.

● V&A   Mus. No. C. 29-1977

209 MUG

Buff base, solid dip. Applied leaf border, topers, trees.
BRISTOL; early 19th Century   Ht. 4¼ins. (11.4cm)
Mrs D. B. Simpson Bequest.
Trees also on previous entry. The central toper known on other jugs of Bristol type.

● V&A   Mus. No. C. 28-1977

210 GOBLET

Buff base, dark dip. Applied vine leaf borders, satyr heads, Bacchanalian putti.

Impressed: *J. BRIGHT J. HAZZARD J. MILSOM E. MELSOM. IN COMMEMORATION OF THE POTTERS WHO RESISTED THE TYRANICAL CONDUCT OF W AND T POW**LL, DECEMBER 4 1818 GOD SAVE THE KING*

BRISTOL (probably John Bright); 1818   Ht. 14ins (35.6cm)

Lit: Pountney 1920 pl. LII. Godden 1966 pl. 78.

Known as the *Bright Goblet*, probably because Bright was the better known of the four potters. Smaller goblets with hunting sprigs are known, such as the three of Bristol type in the Minet Library, Nos. 3/1-3/3.

Lent by Bristol Museum & Art Gallery

211 PUZZLE JUG

Buff base, amber/brown dip. Applied with *The Kill*.

Impressed: *JP 1828*

BRISTOL; 1828   Ht. 7⅞ins. (20cm)

The nozzles of a type found on Swansea creamwares of the early 19th Century.

Lent by the Museum of London   Mus. No. C.67

212 HUNTING JUG

Grey/buff base, matt dark solid dip. Applied with *The Kill*.

Rouletted border.

BRISTOL; c. 1825   Ht. 7½ins. (19cm)

A larger version in Hants Co. Museum Service. Compare the shape with the Wibsey (?) example, dated 1825.

Private Collection

213 HUNTING JUG

Grey base, pale greenish dip. Applied with a hunt.
Rouletted border.
BRISTOL; c. 1825.   Ht. 3ins. (7.8cm)
Transferred from the Museum of Practical Geology, Hermyn Street.
Originally given by Dr H Diamond.

● V&A   Mus. No. 3772-1901

214 HUNTING MUG

Buff base, dark solid dip. Applied with *The Kill*.
Impressed: *JONAS OLDS HANHAM 1840*
BRISTOL; 1840   Ht. 4⅛ins. (10.5cm)
From the Struan Robertson Collection.
Hanham is on the outskirts of Bristol.

Lent by Brighton Museum & Art Gallery

215 INK WELL

Patchy buff/brown.
Inscribed: *Primitive Methodists Chapel 1835*
Mark or owner's name: R^d *Hole Bristol* on base.
BRISTOL; 1835   Ht. 2⅛ins. (5.4cm)
No potter called Hole is recorded. It could be the mark of an unknown
pottery workman, or an owner's name.

Lent by Brighton Museum & Art Gallery

216 TOBACCO JAR

Yellow and cream Bristol-glaze.
Impressed: *ALFRED, EVENS BRISTOL 1869*
BRISTOL (Price or Powell); 1869   Ht. 7ins. (17.8cm)
Lit: Oswald, Hildyard & Hughes 1982 Col. Pl. E.
Exhibited *Ceramics in Bristol. Eight Centuries of Bristol Pottery &
Porcelain*, Bristol Museum 1979
For a salt-glazed piece of similar type, see R. Myer 1930 pl. 207B.
Bristol-glazed money boxes surmounted by miniature jugs are known, as
well as earlier salt-glazed examples, such as that impressed *A. Carter
New Inn* in Salisbury Museum.

Private Collection.

217 LOVING CUP

Yellowish base, amber top, Bristol-glazed. Applied monkeys smoking and gaming.
Mark: *Powell Bristol* (on each side)
BRISTOL (Powell); mid-19th Century.   Ht. 5⅛ins. (13cm)
Lit: Rhoda Edwards 1973 No. 3/11
The monkey sprigs, derived from The Smoking Party by David Teniers the Younger, engraved by T. Caldwell 1798, are more commonly found on Brampton stonewares.

Lent by the Minet Library

BROWNE MUGGS

THE MIDLANDS & NORTH

218 POSSET POT

Light brown overall. Applied (incorrect) Royal Arms.
Inscribed: *Samuel Watkinson Major Sarah his wife Majoress of Nottingham 1700.*
NOTTINGHAM; 1700   Ht. 10½ins. (26.7cm)
Lit: Oswald & Hughes 1974 pl. 90. Wood 1980. Oswald, Hildyard & Hughes 1982 pl. 61.

Lent by Nottingham Castle Museum.   Mus. No. 38.173

219 LOVING CUP

Lustrous dark overall. Incised snailshell decoration, with a flower pot.
Inscribed: *Nottingham January 25 1703.*
NOTTINGHAM; 1703   Ht. 7¼ins. (18.4cm)
Lit: Oswald & Hughes 1974 pl. 91. Wood 1980. Oswald, Hildyard & Hughes 1982 pl. 68.
Shows the *Flower Pot* included in Morley's advertisement of c. 1700.

Lent by Nottingham Castle Museum   Mus. No. 38.72.

220 PIERCED MUG

Patchy lustrous dark brown and tan.
Inscribed: *Nott^{m}: 1703*
NOTTINGHAM; 1703   Ht. 4ins. (10.2cm)
Lit: Godden 1966 pl. 448. Godden 1974 pl. 60.
Compare the *Carved Jug* of Morley's advertisement.
Compare also the piece inscribed *1701 Crich* in Nottingham Castle Museum. These were pierced through the outer wall, the pieces falling through the open bottom.

● V&A   Mus. No. 803-1872

221 PIERCED MUG

Lustrous brown overall.
NOTTINGHAM; c. 1700   Ht. 3¾ins. (9.5cm)
Miss H.M. Spanton Bequest.

● V&A   Mus. No. C.7-1935

222 PIERCED MUG

Lustrous dark overall.
NOTTINGHAM; c. 1700   Ht. 4½ins. (11.4cm)
Given by Lady Lister

● V&A   Mus. No. C.354-1919

223 PiERCED MUG

Dark brown overall
NOTTINGHAM; c. 1700   Ht. 3¾ins. (9.6cm)

● V&A   Mus. No. CIRC. 247-1928

224 JUG

Lustrous orange/brown. Incised tulip.
Inscribed: *April 28th 1702*
DERBYSHIRE (Crich); 1702   Ht. 8½ins. (21.5cm)
From the Glaisher Collection.
Lit: Rackham & Read 1924 pl. 150. Rackham 1935. Oswald & Hughes 1974
pl. 90c. Oswald, Hildyard & Hughes 1982 pl. 59.
Purchased at Fritchley, near Crich.

Lent by the Syndics of the Fitzwilliam Museum   Mus. No. Gl.1227

225 JUG

Lustrous orange/brown. Incised feathery sprays.
Inscribed: *Henry Browne 1704*
Possibly DERBYSHIRE (Crich); 1704   Ht. 10¼ins. (25.4cm)
From the Glaisher Collection. Formerly Bateman and Harland
Collections.
Lit: Rackham 1935.
A label states that it was found at Wirksworth in the mid-19th Century
(five miles from Crich)

Lent by the Syndics of the Fitzwilliam Museum   Mus. No. Gl.1250

226 MUG

Lustrous freckled brown overall. Incised "snail shell' and foliage.
Inscribed: *1700*
Conjoined WR excise mark
NOTTINGHAM; 1700   Ht. 8ins. (20.5cm)
The earliest dated mug of this type, the *Mogg* of Morley's advertisement.
Excavated at Temple Balsall, along with early 18th Century Nottingham
and Staffordshire stonewares.

Lent by the Lady Katherine Leveson Charity

227 MUG WITH TWO HANDLES

Lustrous dark overall. Impressed geometric pattern.
Inscribed: *Iohn Young november 1718*
NÖTTINGHAM; 1718   Ht. 6½ins. (16.5cm)
From the Glaisher Collection. Formerly Sheldon Collection.
Lit: Rackham 1935.

Lent by the Syndics of the Fitzwilliam Museum   Mus. No. Gl.1230

228 MUG

Lustrous brown overall. Rouletting, incised flowers.
Inscribed: *Sarah Hole Novᵇ yᵉ 19ᵗʰ 1720*
NOTTINGHAM; 1720   Ht. 4½ins. (11.4cm)
From the Glaisher Collection. Formerly Tangye Collection.
Lit: Rackham 1935
Compare Oswald, Hildyard & Hughes 1982 pls. 72-5.

Lent by the Syndics of the Fitzwilliam Museum.   Mus. No. Gl.1231

229 FLASK

Translucent oily brown. Rouletted border.
Inscribed: *My Love is pure and shall Endure JB 1723*
NOTTINGHAM; 1723   Ht. 4½ins. (11.5cm)
Lit: Oswald, Hildyard & Hughes 1982 pl. 97
Compare a near duplicate in the Fitzwilliam, inscribed *Joseph Poyne
1723,* Gl.1232.

Private Collection

230 FLASK

Lustrus brown overall. Incised flowers.
Inscribed: *Benjamin Limeburner 1727*
Possibly CRICH; 1727   Ht. 5⅜ins. (13.5cm)
From the Glaisher Collection.
Lit: Rackham 1935
Dr. Glaisher noted that Crich was well-known for lime. Unlike the
previous entry, this flask was evidently intended as a man's spirit flask.
Replacement silver mount.

Lent by the Syndics of the Fitzwilliam Museum   Mus. No. Gl.1251

231 PUNCH BOWL

Lustrous brown overall. Rouletted bands.
Inscribed: *November 20 1726*
NOTTINGHAM; 1726   Diameter: 13ins. (33cm)
Transferred from the Museum of Practical Geology, Jermyn Street.
Originally given by Miss Lakin.

● V&A   Mus. No. 3686-1901

232 PUNCH BOWL

Lustrous brown overall. Incised flowers, rouletted bands.
Inscribed: *Old England For Ever 1750*
NOTTINGHAM; 1750   Ht. 12¾ins. (32.4cm)
Transferred from the Museum of Practical Geology, Jermyn Street.

● V&A   Mus. No. 3687-1901

233 LOVING CUP

Lustrous brown overall. Incised flowers, cut decoration.
Inscribed: *Thomas Smeeton & Mary His Wife 1739*
possibly CRICH; 1739   Ht. 8¼ins. (21cm)
From the Glaisher Collection
Lit: Rackham 1935

Lent by the Syndics of the Fitzwilliam Museum   Mus. No. Gl 1234

234 LOVING CUP

Lustrous brown overall. Incised flowers, rouletting.
Inscribed: *1740* (each side)
NOTTINGHAM; 1740   Ht. 6⅞ins. (17.5cm)
Lit: Honey 1933.
The cross-hatching produced by cutting lines across the helical
rouletting.

● V&A   Mus. No. C. 353-1919

235 LOVING CUP

Lustrous brown overall. Incised geometric decoration, with rouletting
and slip-painted flower sprays.
NOTTINGHAM; c. 1750   Ht. 8½ins. (21.7cm)
Formerly Gautier Collection.
The slip-painting without incised borders. An almost identical example,
dated 1750, sold Christies 16/7/79.

● V&A   Mus. No. C. 412-1928

236 TEACADDY

Lustrous brown. Incised flowers with slip painting, rouletted borders.
Inscribed: *John and Hana Asquith*
Mark: *John Asquith maker 1756*
NOTTINGHAM (John Asquith); 1756   Ht. 3½ins. (8.8cm)
Lit: Wood 1980 pl. 11

Lent by Nottingham Castle Museum   Mus. No. 30. 38

237 TEAPOT & LID

Lustrous brown overall. Incised flowers filled with brown slip.
NOTTINGHAM; c. 1775-1800   Ht. 5½ins. (14cm)
Lit: Wood 1980 pl. 11. Oswald, Hildyard & Hughes 1982 p. 127.
The slip decoration confined by incised lines in the manner of German
stonewares from the Westerwald, with cobalt blue decoration. The
crossed handles and terminals copied from Leeds creamwares.

Lent by Nottingham Castle Museum   Mus. No. 30. 36

238 BOWL

Lustrous brown overall. Breadcrumb and rouletted bands.
NOTTINGHAM; third quarter 18th Century   Diameter: 8⅝ins. (22cm)
Given by Sir George Murray K. B. E.

● V&A   Mus. No. C. 10-1938

239 SPOUTED BOWL

Orange/yellow brown overall. Breadcrumb, straight and zig zag incised
lines.
NOTTINGHAM; third quarter 18th Century.   Ht. 2⅞ins. (7.2cm)
Compare decoration with next entry.

● V&A   Mus. No. C. 303-1927

240 TEAPOT & LID

Lustrous brown overall. Breadcrumb decoration, incised straight and
zig zag lines.
NOTTINGHAM; third quarter 18th Century.   Ht. 5⅛ins. (13cm)
From the Glaisher Collection.
Lit: Rackham 1935
Compare a similar example in Nottingham Castle Museum.

Lent by the Syndics of the Fitzwilliam Museum   Mus. No. G11238

241 LOVING CUP

Lustrous brown overall. Breadcrumb and cut decoration.
NOTTINGHAM; third quarter 18th Century.   Ht. 6⅛ins. (15.6cm)
The cut decoration, known as *Kerbschnitt,* is common on 16th Century
German stonewares.

● V&A   Mus. No. C. 302-1927

242 BEAR CISTERN

Lustrous brown overall. Coat of *grog*.
NOTTINGHAM; third quarter 18th Century.   Ht. 13ins. (33cm)
Nottingham bears are more common as tobacco jars or jugs with heads
as cups. The only dated piece was a jug, with attached ball inscribed
Elizabeth Clarck December ye 25th 1769 (the ball now at Nottingham
Castle Museum).

● V&A   Mus. No. 1180-1864

243 TWO TILES

Lustrous brown overall. Impressed and rouletted decoration.
NOTTINGHAM; second half 18th Century.   5¼ins. (13.4cm) square
Formerly Gollancz Collection.
From Morley's house in Nottingham. Other examples were in the
Campion Collection. For a tile in the Stretton Collection, see Godden
1966 pl. 449. Each tile is decorated with one or two stamps, arranged to
form patterns, that on C. 49-1975 being identical to a stamp on the jug
C. 318-1931.

● V&A   Mus. No. C. 49, 49A-1975

244 JUG

Lustrous brown overall. Incised and rouletted strips, crown and national
emblems.
Inscribed: *GR 1765*
NOTTINGHAM; 1765   Ht. 9⅝ins. (24.5cm)
Lit: Oswald & Hughes 1974 pl. 96. Wood 1980 p. 9.

Lent by Nottingham Castle Museum   Mus. No. 34. 165

245 DOUBLE TEA CADDY

Lustrous brown overall. Moulded with mermaids, impressed diaper
pattern.
Mark or owner's name: *E. H. 1770* on base
NOTTINGHAM or CRICH; 1770   Ht. 5ins. (13cm)
From the Glaisher Collection.
Lit. Rackham 1935. Oswald & Hughes 1974 pl. 104.
Moulded caddies of different design by William Lockett, dated 1755, 1764,
in Nottingham Castle Museum.

Lent by the Syndics of the Fitzwilliam Museum   Mus. No. Gl. 1240

246 INK POT

Lustrous freckled overall.
Inscribed: *Sarah Emminson 1762*
NOTTINGHAM; 1762   Ht. 2¼ins. (5.5cm)
From the Glaisher Collection.
Lit: Rackham 1935

Lent by the Syndics of the Fitzwilliam Museum   Mus. No. Gl. 1239

247 INK POT

Lustrous brown overall.
Inscribed: *Jno Bagshaw Nott^m made y^e 21 May 1783*
NOTTINGHAM; 1783   Diameter: 3⅛ins. (7.8cm)
Mrs. M. B. Sargeant Bequest.
The neck bears traces of lead-glaze lining.

● V&A   Mus. No. C. 26-1967

248 POUNCE POT

Inscribed: *1767*
NOTTINGHAM; 1767   Ht. 3ins. (7.6cm)
Formerly Revelstoke Collection.
Lit: Oswald & Hughes 1974 pl. 104

Lent by Stoke on Trent Museum   Mus. No. 288 P35

249 JUG

Reddish brown overall. Applied, incised, stamped and rouletted
decoration.
Inscribed; *Moses Frooms Levin in Chosely Parish. Fill Me up unto the
Brim When I am out fill me again Nottingham June y^e: 26 1759*
NOTTINGHAM (probably William Lockett); 1759   Ht. 11⅜ins. (28.9cm)
Note that a stamp on the handle is identical to those on the tile
c. 49-1975.

● V&A   Mus. No. C.318-1931

250 MUG

Lustrous brown overall. Applied and incised decoration.
Inscribed: *John Johnson. Schoolmaster. Nottingham. Sepm. ye: 3.1762*
Mark: *Wm Lockett* on base
NOTTINGHAM (William Lockett); 1762   Ht. 7⅜ins. (18.7cm)
Lit: Wood 1980 pl. 9

Lent by Nottingham Castle Museum   Mus. No. 03.27

251 MUG

Lustrous brown overall. Applied, incised, rouletted and impressed decoration.
Inscribed: *Made at Nottingham y^e 17th Day of August A.D. 1771*
NOTTINGHAM (probably William Lockett); 1771   Ht. 6⅞ins. (17.4cm)
Transferred from the Museum of Practical Geology, Jermyn Street.
Originally given by Edmund Percy.
Lit; Blacker 1922 p. 88. Godden 1966 pl. 450.

●V&A   Mus. No. 3688-1901

252 MUG

Lustrous brown overall. Impressed and rouletted decoration.
Inscribed: *G III R. Willm & Mary Bidelle of Staturn in Leicestershire*
Mark: *Moses Colclough ye maker at Nott^m may ye 13th AD 1771*
NOTTINGHAM (Moses Colclough); 1771   Ht. 6ins. (15.3cm)
Lit: Oswald & Hughes 1974 pl. 98

Lent by Nottingham Castle Museum   Mus. No. 58.32

253 MUG

Lustrous brown overall. Applied and incised decoration.
Inscribed: *James Gilbart of Abberstone Made May the 1 at Nottingham AD 1772*
Mark: *Maker Thomas Hough 1772* on base
NOTTINGHAM (Thomas Hough); 1772   Ht. 7ins. (18cm)
Formerly David Hicks Collection.
Lit: Oswald, Hildyard & Hughes 1982 pl. 82.
Apparently the only signed Hough piece. Other pots attributable to Hough are the mug inscribed *T.A. 1772* and the jug inscribed *Adam Woolley 1771* (next entry), both in Nottingham Castle Museum.

Private Collection.

254 JUG

Lustrous brown overall. Applied, incised, impressed and rouletted decoration.
Inscribed: *Adam Woolley of Nott^m made Feb^r y^e 19 1771*
NOTTINGHAM (Thomas Hough); 1771   Ht. 9ins. (22.9cm)
Lit: Wood 1980 pl. 12.

Lent by Nottingham Castle Museum   Mus. No. 30.21

255 MUG

Dark brown overall. Rouletted borders.
Inscribed: *1775 I M Good Ale*
Mark: *Belper. march 30th*, on base.
BELPER; 1775   Ht. 7⅛ins. (18cm)
Formerly Drinkwater, Garner Collections.
Lit: Drinkwater 1939 pl. XII

Lent by Derby Museum

256 PUNCH BOWL

Dark brown overall. Incised and rouletted tulips and diaper.
Inscribed: *H.M.K. Made at Belper May 29th 1775 One more bowl and then* (inside)
BELPER; 1775   Diameter 13½ins. (34.5cm)
Lit: Oswald & Hughes 1974 pl. 97
Illegible inscription on base.

Lent by Derby Museum.

257 CHARGER

Dark brown overall. Incised and rouletted radial strips.
Probably DERBYSHIRE (Belper); c. 1780-1800
Diameter 16¼ins. (41.5cm)
Lit: Wood 1980 pl. 14. Oswald, Hildyard & Hughes 1982 pl. 139.
Brown stoneware dishes are extremely rare, since potters did not attempt to compete with the cheap Staffordshire flatwares.

Lent by Nottingham Castle Museum   Mus. No. 997. 401

258 JAR

Lustrous brown overall.
Inscribed: *H^R E 1799*
Probably BELPER; 1799   Ht. 5¼ins. (13.5cm)
Lit: Oswald, Hildyard & Hughes 1982 pl. 149.
A pair has been noted, suggesting that several may have been made as a wedding present. Compare the later straight-sided jam jar in this exhibition.

Private Collection

259 INK POT

Light brown, patchy. Modelled as the head of an old woman.
Probably DENBY; c. 1830   Ht. 2⅜ins. (6.1cm)
Transferred from the Museum of Practical Geology, Jermyn Street.
A full-figure version, made as a flask, in Brighton Museum.

● V&A   Mus. No. 3768-1901

260 INK POT

Buff overall.
Mark: *SHIPLEY POTTERY,* impressed.
SHIPLEY POTTERY; c. 1830   Length 2⅝ins. (6.6cm)

Lent by Stoke on Trent Museum   Mus. No. 61. P. 53

261 MONEY BOX

Dark brown overall.
Inscribed: *Hannah Sanders Belper Jan 17th 1834*
BELPER; 1834   Ht. 6ins. (15.2cm)
Lit: Oswald & Hughes 1974, pl. 104

Lent by Stoke on Trent Museum   Mus. No. 214. P. 50

262 JUG

Patchy freckled buff base, dark freckled dip. Applied windmill, toper, tree.
Mark: *BOURNE'S Warranted,* impressed
BELPER/DENBY; c.1830   Ht. 4ins. (10.2cm)
Transferred from the Museum of Practical Geology, Jermyn Street.
The sprigs tooled around with a pointed implement.

● V&A   Mus. No. 3692-1901

263 BIRD WHISTLE

Light buff/brown. Applied topers, windmill.
Inscribed: *Joseph Walker Henmore April 14th 1824*
BELPER/DENBY; 1824   Ht. 6⅛ins. (15.5cm)
Lit: Oswald & Hughes 1974 pl. 97. Oswald, Hildyard & Hughes 1982 pl. 123.
Henmoore is near Belper.

Lent by Derby Museum   Mus. No. 472

264 HUNTING JUG

Light speckled buff. Applied windmill, topers, tree, hunt.
Inscribed: *Robert & Lucy Bancroft Derby June 29 1825*
BELPER/DENBY; 1825   Ht. 6ins. (15.4cm)
Formerly Hill Collection.
Lit: Oswald, Hildyard & Hughes 1982 pl. 125
Sprigs tooled around. Note that a Joseph Bancroft, born at Derby 1796, worked as a decorator at Ridgway's.

Private Collection.

265 JUG

Freckled light brown base, darker dip. Applied stag and boar hunt.
BELPER/DENBY; c.1830   Ht. 5⅝ins. (14.3cm)
Mrs. D.B. Simpson Bequest.
Sprigs tooled around. A drab coloured stoneware version in the Fitzwilliam Museum, marked *Phillips Bagster,* datable to c. 1820-25.

● V&A   Mus. No. C. 30-1977

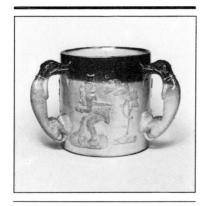

266 LOVING CUP

Freckled light brown base, dark dip. Applied male & female harvesters, Paul Pry, tree, St. George.
DENBY; c. 1840   Ht. 7ins. (17.6cm)
Lit: Blacker 1922 p. 92
Sprigs tooled around.

● V&A   Mus. No. 463-1905

267 HUNTING JUG

Cream base, reddish freckled dip. Applied windmill, topers, trees, hunt, grapevine terminal
BELPER/DENBY; c. 1830-40   Ht. 6⅝ins. (16.8cm)
The sprigs tooled around, the body with iron specks.

Private Collection.

268 HUNTING JUG

Light brown base, lustrous dark dip. Applied trees, topers, hunt.
BELPER/DENBY; c. 1830-40   Ht. 9⅛ins. (23.3cm)
Sprigs tooled around. Note the angled hounds and "rocking" horse with curved base found on other Bourne jugs, such as No. 5/1 in the Minet Library.

Private Collection

269 HUNTING MUG

Light brown base, dark dip. Applied topers, tree, man with horse.
BELPER/DENBY; c. 1830-40   Ht. 5¼ins. (13.3cm)
Sprigs tooled around, iron specked body. Bristol-glazed versions are common, suggesting a long period of production.

Private Collection

270 MUG

Buff base, solid dip. Applied tree and gipsy encampment scenes.
Impressed: *ALEXANDER OGDEN BORN JULY 26 1835*
DENBY; 1835   Ht. 4⅝ins. (11.6cm)
Sprigs tooled around. The gipsy sprig used at Port-Dundas: see
Cruickshank 1983.

Lent by Derby Museum

271 MUG

Light brown overall. Medallions of a building, Charles and John Wesley.
Impressed: *FARNSFIELD WESLEYAN FRIENDLY SOCIETY CENTENARY
OF WESLEYAN METHODISM 1839. THE WORLD IS MY PARISH.
CENTENARY HALL AND MISSION HOUSE LONDON*
DENBY; 1839   Ht. 4⅜ins. (11cm)
Compare a bowl with similar decoration in Denby Pottery Collection,
illustrated Oswald & Hughes 1974 pl. 101. A stoneware Methodist
collection box is in Derby Museum.

Private Collection

272 FLASK

Buff base, dark dip.
Impressed: *IRISH REFORM CORDIAL   DANIEL O'CONNELL ESQ.*
Mark: *BOURNES, POTTERIES DENBY & CODNOR PARK DERBYSHIRE*
DENBY/CODNOR PARK; c. 1835-40   Ht. 8ins. (20.3cm)
Transferred from the Museum of Practical Geology, Jermyn Street.
The inclusion of *Codnor Park* indicates a date after 1833.

● V&A   Mus. No. 3691-1901

273 FLASK

Light brown base, lustrous dark dip.
Impressed: *WILLIAM, IV, TH'S REFORM CORDIAL* *
Mark: *BELPER & DENBY *BOURNES POTTERIES DERBYSHIRE* *
BELPER/DENBY; c. 1832   Ht. 7¾ins. (19.7cm)
Private Collection.

274 DRUG JAR OR SHOP POT

Buff base, watery brown dip. Painted label.
BELPER/DENBY; c. 1830-40   Ht. 7¼ins. (18.5cm)
Compare the Brampton example. Other Denby pots, with original
japanned lids and gilt inscriptions, are in Spalding Gents Association.

Lent by Derby Museum.

275 BOTTLE

Gritty olive/brown overall.
Impressed: *OWEN GROCER SWINDON*
Mark: *J. BOURNE PATENTEE, DENBY & CODNOR PARK POTTERY NEAR
DERBY VITREOUS STONE BOTTLES WARRANTED NOT TO ABSORB*
DENBY/CODNOR PARK; c. 1840-50   Ht. 12ins. (30.5cm)

Private Collection.

276 BLACKING BOTTLE

Grey/buff.
Impressed: *BLACKING BOTTLE JBD 17*
DENBY; probably 1817   Ht. 5¼ins. (13.5cm)
The numeral *17* probably indicates the date, while *JBD* stands for Joseph
Bourne Denby. Bottles marked *Blacking Bottle* were exempt from the
duty in force 1817-34.

Private Collection.

277 BOTTLE

Matt olive/brown.
Impressed: *EX*
DERBYSHIRE (possibly Denby); 1817-34   Ht. 5¾ins. (14.5cm)
EX indicated that duty had been paid. The shape is probably a ginger
beer bottle, which later developed the characteristic sharp shoulder and
bulbous lip.

Private Collection.

278 INK BOTTLE

Olive/amber overall.
Impressed: *DEACON & MORRELL Fleet-street, London*
DERBYSHIRE; early 19th Century   Ht. 4ins. (10.2cm)
Deacon & Morrell listed at Pen & Quill Warehouse, 149 Fleet St. c. 1807-c.
1820. Another battered example in Museum of London.

Lent by Museum of London   Mus. No. 31. 6

279 INK BOTTLE

Freckled brown overall.
Label for *Walkden's Brilliant Scarlet Ink*
probably DERBYSHIRE; late 19th Century   Ht. 1¾ins. (4.5cm)
The last stoneware ink bottle shape, made in Derbyshire and London in
huge quantities.

Private Collection.

280 BOTTLE

Lustrous brown overall.
Label for *Standard Brand, Superior Brunswick Black*
Mark: *Bourne Denby* in oval
DENBY; late 19th Century   Ht. 5½ins. (14cm)
The half pint Brunswick Black Bottle was listed by Doulton and Stiff in
1873 at 13/- (65P) and 14/- (70P) per gross. Denby products might have
been cheaper.

Private Collection.

281 PAIR OF LIONS

Lustrous dark brown overall, with white clay details.
Probably DERBYSHIRE; early 19th Century   Ht. 11⅝ins. (29.5cm)
Mrs. Lucie Aldridge Bequest.
A similar lion in Fitzwilliam Museum. Another at Keighley Museum, with
a possible Yorkshire provenance.

● V&A   Mus. No. C.7 & A-1975

282 FIGURE OF ST. GEORGE

Patchy buff/brown overall.
Probably DERBYSHIRE (Brampton); first half 19th Century
Ht. 7⅞ins. (20cm)
Given by H. Grimsdale
Sprigs of St. George are frequently found on Denby mugs and jugs, but this figure is apparently unique.

● V&A   Mus. No. C.456-1940

283 FIGURE OF A DOG

Honey coloured.
BRAMPTON; second quarter 19th Century   Ht. 3ins. (7.6cm)

Lent by Derby Museum   Mus. No. 1319

284 FIGURE OF A COW

Honey coloured.
BRAMPTON; second quarter 19th Century   Ht. 1⅞ins. (4.8cm)

Lent by Derby Museum   Mus. No. 1649-3

285 LOVING CUP

Lustrous brown overall. Incised and rouletted decoration.
Inscribed: *George & Sarah Webster Married Feby 25th 1805*
BRAMPTON/CHESTERFIELD; 1805   Ht. 9ins. (22.8cm)

● V&A   Mus. No. CIRC. 248-1928

286 LOVING CUP

Dark lustrous overall, with lead glaze lining. Applied monkeys gaming and smoking, ploughing scene.
Impressed: *GEORGE & LYDIA DOE BRAMPTON*
BRAMPTON; c. 1830   Ht. 9ins. (22.8cm)
The monkey sprig, after The Smoking Party by David Teniers the Younger, engraved by T. Caldwell 1798, is also found on the Powell loving cup in this exhibition.

Lent by Derby Museum   Mus. No. 1312

287 LOVING CUP

Lustrous brown overall. Stamped and incised foliage.
Inscribed: *With caution walk our fruitful way Our work shall soon be done Let friendship reign while here we stay And eveil speak of none 1849*
BRAMPTON; 1849   Ht. 9½ins. (24cm)

Lent by Stoke on Trent Museum   Mus. No. 125.P.38

288 LOVING CUP

Honey colour. Applied sprays, scrolls, vine leaf border, shooting scenes.
Impressed: *LLEWELLYN JEWITT WINSTER, HALL, APRIL 3, 1871*
BRAMPTON; 1871   Ht. 9¼ins. (23.4cm)
One of a pair (see next entry) presented to Jewitt, and noted in his *Ceramic Art of Great Britain*, 1878, but without mention of which pottery made them. They demonstrate perfectly the two types of Brampton ware: white refined body with honey coloured glaze, and coarse grey body with lustrous brown glaze and a necessary lead glaze lining.

● V&A   Mus. No. C.2-1982

289 LOVING CUP

Lustrous brown overall, with lead glaze lining. Applied sprays, scrolls, vine leaf border, shooting scenes.
Impressed: *LLEWELLYN JEWITT. WINSTER HALL. APRIL 3 1871*
BRAMPTON; 1871   Ht. 9¼ins. (23.4cm)
Coarse grey body.

● V&A   Mus. No. C. 2A-1982

290 TOBY JUG

Honey coloured.
BRAMPTON; c.1840   Ht. 8½ins. (21.5cm)
Compare a marked Oldfield example, differing in detail, in Sheffield
Museum, illustrated Oswald, Hildyard & Hughes 1982 pl. 113.

Lent by Derby Museum   Mus. No. 698-2-1977

291 PUZZLE JUG

Dark brown overall. Pierced and rouletted decoration.
Inscribed: *Gentlemen come try your skill I'll hold a water if you will You
don't drink this liquor all Unless you spill or let some fall*
Mark: *J^{no} Wright Maker 1775*
BRAMPTON (John Wright, Wheatbridge Pottery); 1775
Ht. 6⅞ins. (17.5cm)
Lit: Oswald & Hughes 1974 pl.104. Oswald, Hildyard & Hughes 1982 pl.104.
For a similar example, inscribed *John Wright, maker, Chesterfield 1775*,
see Godden 1974 pl. 70.

Lent by Derby Museum   Mus. No. 707-1939

292 PUZZLE JUG

Lustrous dark brown overall. Pierced and rouletted.
Inscribed: *Fany While Her Jug 1788*
DERBYSHIRE OR YORKSHIRE; 1788   Ht. 8½ins. (21.2cm)
Given by Miss Amy E Tomes.
Comparison with a puzzle jug inscribed *John Gould Dunnington 1780*,
sold Sothebys 1978, suggests that this might be a Yorkshire product.
Dunnington is in Yorkshire.

● V&A   Mus. No. C. 105-1937

293 PUZZLE JUG

Lustrous dark brown overall.
Inscribed: *Here you may Drink and take y^r fill But four Pence pay if you
do Spill Novr 5 1802*
DERBYSHIRE (probably Brampton); 1802   Ht. 8ins. (20.5cm)
Handle junctions apparently applied with lead(?) glaze.

Private Collection.

294 PUZZLE JUG

Brown overall.
Inscribed: *Come Gentlemen and try your skill* etc. *March 23 1823* (on base)
BRAMPTON; 1823   Ht. 6¾ins. (7.1cm)
Compare a similar jug from the Pitt Rivers Collection, sold Sothebys 14/3/78, dated *March 20th 1823,* probably by the same potter. A more elaborate jug at Brighton Museum dated *Sept. 22 1823*

Private Collection.

295 PUZZLE JUG

Honey colour. Applied tree, topers, windmill, Vicar & Moses.
BRAMPTON; c. 1835   Ht. 8ins. (20.5cm)
Compare a honey-coloured puzzle jug with different sprigs at Leicester Museum, impressed *R. Gilry 1837*

Private Collection.

296 PUZZLE JUG

Dark brown overall.
Inscribed: *Come Gentlemen come try your skill* etc. *Eastmoor Pottery, Brampton, Aug. 7 1837*
BRAMPTON (Eastmoor Pottery); 1837   Ht. 8¾ins. (22.2cm)
Lit: Oswald, Hildyard & Hughes 1982 pl. 115.

Lent by Derby Museum.

297 TOBACCO BOX, CANDLESTICK AND STAND

Honey coloured. Moulded with dolphins and Venus on Shell.
BRAMPTON; c. 1830-35   Ht. 7⅛ins. (18cm)

Lent by Derby Museum   Mus. No. 698-7-1977

298 TOBACCO POT AND CANDLESTICK

Dark brown overall. Applied topers, windmill, hunt.
Impressed: *Richard Wood Burslem*
Incised: *Richard Wood*. On base: *August 3rd 1833*
Probably BRAMPTON; 1833   Ht. 7½ins. (19cm)

Lent by Stoke on Trent Museum   Mus. No. 115.P.38

299 TOBACCO POT (WITH INNER LID)

Lustrous brown/buff. Applied Hercules & the Lion, flower basket,
cornucopia, Royal Arms.
Probably BRAMPTON; mid 19th Century
Ht. 6½ins. (16.5cm)

Lent by Derby Museum   Mus. No. 1317

300 BUTTER POT

Pinky buff, frit lined. Applied floral border and handles.
Probably BRAMPTON; mid-19th Century.   Ht. 2¾ins. (7cm)
Transferred from the Museum of Practical Geology, Jermyn Street.

● V&A   Mus. No. 3990-1901

301 EGG CUP STAND

Lustrous honey colour.
BRAMPTON; second quarter 19th Century   Ht. 6ins. (15.2cm)
Another example at Derby Museum.

Lent by Brighton Museum & Art Gallery   Mus. No. 321097

302 TOAST RACK

Honey colour. Moulded with heads of Q. Victoria and Prince Albert.
BRAMPTON; c. 1840   Ht. 3⅝ins. (9.2cm)
Given by Miss M. Dawson

● V&A   Mus. No. C.3-1935

303 CRADLE WITH CHILD

Honey colour.
BRAMPTON; c. 1830-40   L. 5ins. (12.7cm)
Probably a child's toy.

● V&A   Mus. No. CIRC. 1144-1967

304 HUNTING JUG

Buff base, lustrous solid brown dip. Applied with *The Kill,* vine leaf
border. Moulded mask spout.
BRAMPTON; c. 1840   Ht. 8⅝ins. (22cm)
Mask jugs, often with greyhound handles, may be dated by an example
bearing heads of Q. Victoria & Prince Albert, commemorating their
marriage in 1840.

Lent by Derby Museum   Mus. No. 681-19-1937

305 FLASK

Lustrous dark brown overall. Moulded with heads of Q. Victoria and
Duchess of Kent.
BRAMPTON; c. 1837.   Ht. 8½ins. (21.6cm)
Another example in Struan Robertson Collection, Brighton Museum.
A larger version with titles beneath the heads in Derby Museum, No.
573-1-1976. Similar flask inKeighley Museum is apparently a local
product. Lead-glazed versions also known.

Lent by Derby Museum   Mus. No. 681-12-1937

306 MONEY BOX

Lustrous dark brown overall.
Probably BRAMPTON; early 19th Century   Ht. 5¼ins. (12.7cm)
The more common later honey-coloured examples often sprigged and
inscribed. Money was extracted by breaking the pot.

Private Collection.

307 JAR

Lustrous dark brown overall, lined with lead glaze.
Probably BRAMPTON; mid-19th Century   Ht. 6⅝ins. (17cm)
The standard form of Derbyshire jam jar, produced in vast numbers.
Similar marked Bourne jars, olive brown coloured, are known. A
correspondent in *Pottery Gazette* 1880 noted that "The jam season is now
at its height, and . . . . . the quantity of jars, both large and small, going
off (from Chesterfield) is very considerable".

Private Collection.

308 TEAPOT

Lustrous dark brown overall, frit lined.
Probably CHESTERFIELD/BRAMPTON AREA; second half 19th
Century.   Ht. 10ins. (25.5cm)

Lent by Derby Museum   Mus. No. 749-1-1980

309 TEAPOT

Dark brown overall. Applied flower sprays, rosettes. Frit lined.
Impressed: *C. M. S. 1894*
Probably CHESTERFIELD/BRAMPTON AREA; 1894.
Ht. 4ins. (10.2cm)
Formerly Drinkwater Collection.
Lit: Drinkwater 1939.

● V&A   Mus. No. C. 62-1982

310 HANDLED POT, OR PORRINGER

Lustrous tan overall.
CHESTERFIELD/BRAMPTON AREA; late 18th-early 19th Century.
Ht. 3⅞ins. (9.9cm)
Given by Mrs Hemming.
Examples with lead glaze lining probably date from c. 1825 onwards.
The shape, described in the c. 1900 Pearson's catalogue as a *Porringer*,
was probably a general purpose pot. Some have spouts on the left of the
handle.

● V&A   Mus. No. C. 342-1930

311 WET DRUG JAR

Dark brown overall.
Possibly ILKESTON; early 19th Century   Ht. 6⅛ins. (15.6cm)
A similar example in the British Museum, Mus. No. 1957-12-1-13,
impressed *Syr: R. HAM NI.* Five plain examples in the Wellcome
Collection, some with metal caps on the spouts.

Lent by Derby Museum   Mus. No. 111-1974

312 COFFEE POT

Lustrous dark brown overall. Applied flower sprays, fern leaves. Lead
glaze lined.
Probably CHESTERFIELD/BRAMPTON AREA; mid-19th Century
Ht. 8⅝ins. (21.8cm)
Other examples in Derby Museum, Nottingham Castle Museum, with
various designs.

Private Collection.

313 COFFEE POT

Lustrous dark brown overall, lead glaze line. Applied hunting and
shooting scenes.
Probably ALFRETON; mid-19th Century   Ht. 7½ins. (19cm)
Lit: Oswald & Hughes 1974 pl. 101. Oswald, Hildyard & Hughes 1982
pl. 140.
Found on the site of Alfreton Pottery in 1878, and tentatively attributed.
It is not a waster.

Lent by Derby Museum   Mus. No. 876-1939

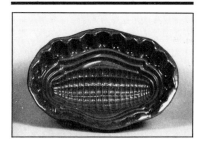

314 JELLY MOULD

Lustrous dark brown overall.
Probably BRAMPTON; first half 19th Century   L. 8¾ins. (22cm)
Smaller sizes, such as Minet Library No. 1/16, have been noted.
The absence of a lead glaze lining suggests an early date, although not all
Brampton potteries lined their wares.

Private Collection

315 COLLANDER

Dark brown overall.
Probably BRAMPTON; mid-19th Century   Diameter 6ins. (15.3cm)
For an earlier example with rouletting and lug handles, see Oswald,
Hildyard & Hughes 1982 pl. 145. Jewitt 1878 mentions that S&H Briddon
and M. Knowles & Son made *cullenders,* but other potteries undoubtedly
produced them as well.

Private Collection

316 MINIATURE HASH POT

Lustrous brown overall. Lead glaze lining.
Inscribed: *H. W. December 15 1823*
Probably BRAMPTON; 1823   Ht. 2¾ins. (7cm)
Perhaps a christening present. This is the earliest dated pot with a lead
glaze lining.

Lent by Derby Museum

317 PIPKIN OR SAUCE POT

Lustrous dark brown overall. Lead glaze lining.
Probably BRAMPTON; second quarter 19th Century
Ht. 6⅝ins. (16.8cm)
Other examples with rouletting in Derby Museum. Jewitt 1878 mentions
that M. Knowles & Son and Oldfield & Co. made *Sauce Pots.*

Private Collection

318 SHOP POT

Lustrous dark brown overall. Lead glaze lining. Applied vine leaves, pre-Victoria Royal Arms and label.
Probably BRAMPTON; second quarter 19th Century
Ht. 7⅝ins. (18.8cm)
Compare the Lambeth and Denby versions.
Private Collection.

319 BARREL

Dark reddish brown overall. Applied vine leaf borders, lions, Prince of Wales Feathers, pre-Victoria Royal Arms, label.
BRAMPTON; c. 1830-40   Ht. 13⅞ins. (35.2cm)
The Arms and Feathers continued in use long after Q. Victoria's accession. The earliest sprigged Brampton wares date from the 1820s, but a similar barrel with busts of Wiliam IV and Queen Adelaide suggests a date in the 1830s. Figured barrels were made throughout the 19th Century.
Private Collection.

320 SPIRIT BOTTLE

Lustrous dark brown overall. Rouletted bands.
BRAMPTON; early 19th Century.   Ht. 12⅞ins. (32.7cm)
Lead glaze around handle junctions. Blistered body. About 1 gallon capacity.
Private Collection

321 SPIRIT BOTTLE

Greenish Bristol or lead glaze over lustrous brown base.
Impressed: *THO^S MARWOOD WINE & SPIRIT MERCHANT SLINGSBY I GALL*
Incised: *D 319*
Perhaps BRAMPTON; mid-19th Century   Ht. 12¼ins. (31.2cm)
The liquid glaze not unlike the lead glaze dipping on Oldfield stonewares.
Known as *Slab-Sealed Group,* after the serrated-edged label bearing the name: many bottles were made for firms in East Yorkshire or

continued on next page

321 *continued*

Lincolnshire, although one for a Chesterfield firm suggests that they are Derbyshire rather than Yorkshire products. Slingsby is near Malton in the North Riding.

Private Collection

322 PORTER BOTTLE

Lustrous brown overall. Lead glaze lined.
Impressed: *H & R HILDYARD W & PORTER MERCHANTS BRIGG*
Probably DERBYSHIRE; mid-19th Century   Ht. 9ins. (23cm)
Standard porter bottle shape, often found with greyish liquid glaze (see previous entry). Henry & Robert D'Arcy Hildyard owned a wines & spirits business in Bigby Street, Brigg, in the 1850s, Henry being listed alone in 1861.

Private Collection

323 SOUSE POT

Lustrous dark brown overall. Lined with lead glaze.
Rouletted band.
CHESTERFIELD/BRAMPTON AREA; second half
19th Century   Ht. 7ins. (17.8cm)

Lent by Derby Museum   Mus. No. 573-3-1976

324 TEAPOT

Honey colour. Moulded as a man with top hat.
Mark: *S & H BRIDDON*
BRAMPTON (S&H Briddon); c. 1840
Lit: Oswald, Hildyard & Hughes 1982 Col.Pl.H

Lent by Derby Museum

325 TEA CADDY

Honey colour. Moulded with scrolls and grotesques.
Impressed: *GREEN TEA*
BRAMPTON; second quarter 19th Century   Ht. 6¼ins. (16cm)
For a marked S&H Briddon example, showing slight differences in the
mould, see Askey 1981 p. 59.

Lent by Derby Museum   Mus. No. 698-4-1977

326 TOBACCO BOX WITH INNER LID

Honey colour. Moulded with pig-stealing and topers.
BRAMPTON (S&H Briddon); c. 1840
The unglazed inner lid with fleur-de-lys finial, sometimes used on the
outer lid. Marked examples in Fitzwilliam Museum and elsewhere.

Private Collection

327 TOBACCO BOX

Honey colour. Moulded with a cottage and trees.
BRAMPTON (probably S&H Briddon); c. 1840   Ht. 4½ins. (11.5cm);
A marked piece, larger and with slight mould differences, in Derby
Museum.

Private Collection

328 NEPTUNE JUG

Mark: *S & H BRIDDON*
BRAMPTON (S&H Briddon); c. 1840. Ht. 6⅞ins. (17.5cm)
Two other examples in Derby Museum

Lent by Derby Museum   Mus. No. 1642

329 GAME POT

Dark brown overall. Lined with slip and lead glaze.
Mark: *S & H BRIDDON*
BRAMPTON (S&H Briddon); c. 1830   Ht. 8½ins. (21.6cm)

Lent by Derby Museum   Mus. No. 481-1

330 BASKET

Honey colour.
Mark: *. . . H BRIDDON 2*
BRAMPTON (S&H Briddon); c. 1840   Ht. 4⅞ins. (12.4cm)

● V&A   Mus. No. C. 802-1917

331 BASKET

Honey colour.
BRAMPTON (S&H Briddon); c. 1840   Ht. 6ins. (15.4cm)
For a marked example, see Oswald, Hildyard & Hughes 1982 pl. 128.
Another in Derby Museum.

Private Collection.

332 SUGAR POT

Honey colour
Mark: *S & H BRIDDON*
BRAMPTON (S&H Briddon); c. 1840   Ht. 4½ins. (10.8cm)
A matching teapot in Derby Museum.

Lent by Stoke on Trent Museum   Mus. No. 51-P-54

333 SNUFFER

Honey colour. Modelled as a grotesque creature.
BRAMPTON; c. 1840   Ht. 3⅛ins. (7.3cm)

Lent by Brighton Museum & Art Gallery   Mus. No. 321151

334 FLASK

Greenish lead glazed base, lustrous brown top. Moulded as Q. Victoria.
Mark: *OLDFIELD & CO. MAKERS*
BRAMPTON (Oldfield & Co.); c. 1837   Ht. 11⅝ins. (29.5cm)

Lent by Derby Museum   Mus. No. 1326

335 FLASK

Greenish lead glazed base, lustrous brown top. Moulded as man on
barrel.
Mark: *OLDFIELD & Co. MAKERS*
BRAMPTON (Oldfield & Co.); c. 1835-40   Ht. 10½ins. (27cm)
From the Glaisher Collection.
Lit: Rackham 1935

Lent by the Syndics of the Fitzwilliam Museum   Mus. No. Gl. 1253

336 JUG

Honey colour. Moulded as a cottage.
BRAMPTON (perhaps Oldfield & Co.); c. 1840   Ht. 8⅛ins. (20.5cm)
Several sizes are known, as well as enamelled earthenware versions.
The only Brampton firm stated by Jewitt 1878 to be producing *cottage
jugs* was Oldfield & Co.

Private Collection.

337 TOBACCO BOX

Lustrous dark brown overall. Moulded with topers.
Impressed: *IOHN & ELIZABETH FLINT 1839*
BRAMPTON (perhaps Oldfield & Co.); 1839   Ht. 5ins. (13cm)
An identical but honey coloured version, impressed *SAMUEL, YATES*
APRIL 21st 1835 has been noted. The grouped impressed asterisks
beneath these inscriptions may possibly be an Oldfield characteristic.

Private Collection

338 INK POT

Honey colour. Applied rose, shamrock & thistle.
Impressed: *M*A. COOPER 1838*
BRAMPTON (perhaps Oldfield & Co.); 1838   Ht. 2⅛ins. (5.4cm)
Note the grouped asterisks.

Private Collection

339 FIGURE OF GREYHOUND

Honey colour.
BRAMPTON (possibly Oldfield & Co.); mid-19th Century
Ht. 5⅛ins. (13cm)
Given by Mrs Francis Buckley.
Jewitt 1878 noted that Oldfield & Co. made greyhounds.

● V&A   Mus. No. C.195-1913

340 MUG

Grey base, dark lustrous dip. Applied AR medallion and crowns.
STAFFORDSHIRE (Burslem); c. 1700-10.   Ht. 4¾ins. (12cm)
Lit: Oswald, Hildyard & Hughes 1982 pl. 156.
For a mug with identical crowns excavated at Burslem, see Mountford
1971 pl. 6

Lent by the Trustees of the British Museum   Mus. No. F42

341 MUG

Buff base, freckled dip.
WR excise in oval.
STAFFORDSHIRE (probably Burslem); c. 1700-10   Ht. 5⅜ins. (13.7cm)
Lit: Mountford 1971 pl. 244
Excavated at site of Crown Staffordshire China works, Fenton.
Nominal pint capacity.

Lent by Stoke on Trent Museum   Mus. No. 207 P 1979

342 MUG

Lustrous brown overall. Geometric rouletted decoration.
STAFFORDSHIRE (Burslem); early 18th Century   Ht. 8⅛ins. (20.6cm)
Lit: Mountford 1971 pl. 8.
Excavated at George Inn, Burslem in 1929. For similar mugs with AR
excise and rouletted stylised tulips, made in Staffordshire and
Nottingham, see Mountford 1971 pl. 10 and Oswald, Hildyard & Hughes
1982 pl. 62.

Lent by Stoke-on-Trent Museum   Mus. No. 642 P 45

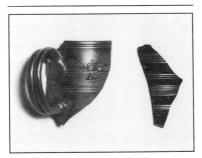

343 MUG FRAGMENTS

Tan with oily sheen, and dark brown.
AR excise.
STAFFORDSHIRE (Burslem); c. 1700-10
Given by Bernard Rackham
Excavated on the site of the George Inn, Burslem.

● V&A   Mus. No. C.161, 161A-1929

344 MUG

Buff base, patchy brown dip with oily sheen.
AR excise mark.
STAFFORDSHIRE (Burslem)   Ht. 3⅞ins. (9.8cm)
Given by G. J. V. Bemrose.
Excavated on the site of the George Inn, Burslem, and evidently a
waster. A false bottom is provided to give short measure.

● V&A   Mus. No. C.15-1932

345 MUG

Buff base, lustrous dark freckled dip.
STAFFORDSHIRE; c. 1700   Ht. 2½ins. (6.4cm)
Transferred from the Museum of Practical Geology, Jermyn Street.
Lit: Honey 1933.
Compare treacle-coloured lead glazed versions in the V&A,
Mus. Nos. 2090, 2091-1901.

● V&A   Mus. No. 2092-1901

346 CAPUCHINE

Buff base, lustrous dark dip.
STAFFORDSHIRE; c. 1700   Ht. 2½ins. (6.4cm)
Given by Mrs Hemming.
Lit: Honey 1933
Excavated in 1912 in London Wall. Compare the Fulham capuchine, and
the pierced Nottingham version, Oswald, Hildyard & Hughes 1982 pl. 66.

● V&A   Mus. No. C.343-1930

347 CRADLE

Buff base, patchy brown dip.
Inscribed: *THOMAS SMITHE HISS CRADDLE*
Probably STAFFORDSHIRE; mid-18th Century   L. 4⅜ins. (11cm)
Mrs Sargeant Bequest. Formerly Drinkwater Collection.
Lit: Drinkwater 1939 pl. XII. English Ceramic Circle Exh. 1948.
Cradles, common is slipware, are otherwise unknown in stoneware. This
was perhaps a one-off piece.

● V&A   Mus. No. C.27-1967

348 CAPUCHINE

Grey with marbled black and brown streaks.
FRANCIS PLACE; c. 1678-94   Ht. 2½ins. (6.4cm)
Transferred from the Museum of Practical Geology, Jermyn Street.
Originally given by Sir A Wollaston Franks KCB.
Formerly Horace Walpole Collection, Strawberry Hill.
Lit: Tyler 1971 pp. 42-4. Tyler 1972 pl. 156.
Exhibited *Horace Walpole & Strawberry Hill*, Orleans Gallery 1980.
Shown with 18th Century case. As a capable artist and engraver Francis

continued on next page

348 *continued*

Place may well have thrown and fired his stonewares himself. Though based at York, Place seems to have had his pottery at Dinsdale, Co Durham. Other examples in Fitzwilliam Museum and British Museum.

● V&A   Mus. No. 4762-1901

349 COFFEE POT

Lustrous dark brown overall.
YORKSHIRE (Wibsey); c. 1820-30   Ht. 7⅛ins. (18cm)
Lit: G. Wilkinson 1981

Lent by Keighley Museum

350 TOBACCO BOX

Dark overall. Moulded with lion, dog finial.
YORKSHIRE (Wibsey); c. 1830   Ht. 4¾ins. (12cm)
Lit: G. Wilkinson 1981

Lent by Keighley Museum

351 PUZZLE JUG

Lustrous brown overall. Two moulded frogs inside.
Probably YORKSHIRE (Wibsey); c. 1830   Ht. 6¾ins. (17.2cm)
An identical jug, with sprigged decoration, inscribed *Joseph Bates 1829*, illustrated Godden 1974 pl. 72. No puzzle jugs with pierced double spouts are at Keighley Museum, but the shape is also unknown elsewhere. Note the frogs, which seem peculiar to Yorkshire stoneware.

Private Collection.

352 JUG

Lustrous reddish brown. Lead glaze lined. Applied sportsmen and dogs, flanked by wigged man with pipe, and toper. Vine scroll border.
Inscribed: J. Walker March 14th*. 1825*
Probably YORKSHIRE (Wibsey); 1825   Ht. 7⅞ins. (20cm)
Compare the similar jug impressed *NOTTINGHAM REVIEW OFFICE 1828* in Nottingham Castle Museum, Oswald, Hildyard & Hughes 1982 pl. 168. The standing topers seem peculiar to Yorkshire stonewares, but are known on Staffordshire Pratt-type wares of earlier in the 19th Century.

Private Collection.

353 MUG

Brown overall, lined with slip and lead glaze. Applied topers, and rouletting. Frog inside.
YORKSHIRE (Wibsey or Eccleshill); c. 1830-40.   Ht. 6½ins. (17cm)
Lit: Oswald, Hildyard & Hughes 1982 pl. 167
See previous entry for similar sprigs, which appear on an Eccleshill coffee pot at Keighley Museum. Note the rouletting with *square* holes, peculiar to Yorkshire wares.

Private Collection

354 SHAVING MUG

Honey coloured base, solid dip. Applied topers, vine leaf border.
YORKSHIRE (Eccleshill); mid-19th Century.   Ht. 6⅛ins. (15.5cm)
The two toper sprigs on a massive jug at Keighley Museum, illustrated Oswald, Hildyard & Hughes 1982 pl. 164.

Lent by Keighley Museum

355 MUG

Lustrous dark brown overall. Applied pheasants and quails, one with moulded title *CHINESE PHEASANTS*.
Impressed: SAM^l *TURNER HALIFAX 1835*
YORKSHIRE (Wibsey or Eccleshill)   Ht. 4ins. (10.2cm)
Possibly an early product of Eccleshill, which was established about 1835-7. The *Chinese Pheasants* perhaps adapted from a transfer-print.

Lent by Keighley Museum

356 PUZZLE JUG

Lustrous brown overall. Lead glaze lined. Applied ivy leaves, topers and Cupid & Psyche.
YORKSHIRE (Eccleshill); c.1840   Ht. 9¼ins. (23.5cm)
Severall Eccleshill pieces at Keighley Museum have the standing toper flanked by ivy leaves, while the angular shape is also found on an Eccleshill coffee pot. The Cupid & Psyche sprig is found on Staffordshire bone chinas of the 1820s, but note that the Eccleshill Pottery was established with Staffordshire workmen *and moulds*.

Private Collection

357 COFFEE POT

Matt lustrous tan/dark brown overall. Lined with slip and lead glaze. Applied lion and dogs or cubs, lioness encircled by snake.
YORKSHIRE (Eccleshill); c.1840-50.   Ht. 10⅜ins. (16.4cm)
Identical sprigs on several Eccleshill pieces at Keighley Museum, but otherwise unknown on stoneware. They have been noted on Staffordshire lilac-ground bone chinas of c.1825-30, and may have the same source as the Cupid & Psyche (previous entry). The ovoid body paralleled on a cistern at Keighley: see G. Wilkinson 1981 p. 24.

Private Collection

358 PUZZLE JUG

Light brown base, dark dip.
Possibly YORKSHIRE; mid-19th Century   Ht. 8⅛ins. (20.7cm)
The geometric piercing is reminiscent of Burton-in-Lonsdale slipwares and stoneware (usually clear Bristol-glazed). No other pieces of this type have been noted.

● V&A   Mus. No. 326-1854

359 TOBACCO JAR

Buff base, freckled dip. Applied topers, windmill, gesticulating boors.
Probably LIVERPOOL; early 19th Century   Ht. 3⅞ins. (9.8cm)
Note the sprig of gesticulating boors, apparently peculiar to Liverpool wares: see Alan Smith 1970 pls. 91-6.

Lent by Merseyside Co. Museums   Mus. No. 57-178-17

360 HUNTING JUG

Buff base, dark dip. Applied toper, tree, windmill, gesticulating boors, shepherd & dog, hunt.
Probably LIVERPOOL; early 19th Century   Ht. 7½ins. (19cm)
Note the sprig of gesticulating boors: see previous entry.

Lent by Nottingham Castle Museum

361 GOBLET

Buff base, brown dip. Applied topers, windmill. Rouletted bands.
Perhaps LIVERPOOL or BRISTOL; early 19th Century
Ht. 6ins. (15.2cm)
Two goblets of identical shape in Minet Library have sprigs of Bristol type, but the shape may have been made at Liverpool as well.

Lent by Merseyside Co. Museums.   Mus. No. 50-139-13

362 COCKLE POT

Light greenish glaze, probably Bristol-type.
Inscribed: *Mrs. Rowley Lancaster 1839*
Possibly LIVERPOOL; 1839   Ht. 14¼ins. (36.3cm)
Given by J. R. Barwell
Steam was passed throught the spout and thence through perforations in the floor of the pot, cooking the cockles in the process. Earthenware examples are known.

● V&A   Mus. No. C.158 &A-1981

363 TOBACCO JAR

Buff overall. Applied farm with horse & trap, feeding chickens, cottage and swans, toper, hunt.
Impressed: *E A. ATKINS*
Inscribed: *1820*
SCOTTISH (Glasgow, Caledonian Pottery); 1820.   Ht. 7⅛ins. (18cm)
An identical cottage & swans sprig appears on the giant jug in Glasgow Museum, marked *W. MURRAY Caledonian Pottery 1828*.

Private Collection.

364 HUNTING JUG

Buff base, freckled dip. Applied trees, windmill, topers, hunt.
SCOTTISH (Glasgow, probably Port-Dundas); mid-19th Century
Ht. 7¾ins. (19.7cm)
Formerly Tait Collection.
The three topers around a table appears on a demijohn in the Smith
Inst., Stirling, attributed to Port-Dundas or Caledonian Pottery, dated
1848.

● V&A   Mus. No. C.65-1981

365 HUNTING JUG

Dark brown overall. Applied toper with *Old Will 1761*, three men at table
tree, hunt.
SCOTTISH (Glasgow, probably Port-Dundas); mid-19th Century
Ht. 8¼ins. (21cm)

Lent by the Museum of London   Mus. No. A273777

366 BEAN POT

Buff base, patchy tan dip. Applied ploughmen & horses, hunt.
Rouletted bands.
SCOTTISH (possibly Port-Dundas); mid-19th Century
Ht. 9ins. (22.8cm)
For rouletted bean pots, see Cruickshank 1983. Also made by Milne &
Cornwall of Portobello. None of these have sprigged decoration.

Private Collection.

367 HUNTING JUG

Light brown base, dark solid dip. Applied topers, hunt.
Mark: PORT-DUNDAS POTTERY C^{oy} GLASGOW, in oval. *1 pint*
SCOTTISH (Glasgow, Port-Dundas); late 19th Century
Ht. 5¼ins. (13.3cm)
Sprigs copied from Doulton. Note flaring neck, typical of late
Port-Dundas jugs.

Private Collection.

BIBLIOGRAPHY

Derek Askey, *Stoneware Bottles,* Brighton 1981

K. J. Barton, *The Barton Collection of Earthenware Pottery,* Guernsey Museum 1982

Mavis Bimson, 'John Dwight', *ECC Transactions* Vol. 5, pt. 2, 1961

J. F. Blacker, *The ABC of English Salt-Glaze Stoneware,* London 1922

R. J. Charleston & Donald Towner, *English Ceramics 1580-1830,* Commem. Cat. ECC 1927-77, London, 1977.

Dennis Cockell, 'Some Finds of Pottery at Vauxhall Cross, London', *ECC Trans* Vol. 9 pt.2, 1974

V. R. Christophers, D. C. Haselgrove, O. H. J. Pearcey, *The Fulham Pottery,* Fulham & Hammersmith Hist. Soc. Occ. Paper 1, 1974

Graeme Cruickshank, *Scottish Saltglaze,* Scot. Pot. Studies No. 2, 1983

John Drinkwater, 'Some Notes on English Salt-Glaze Brown Stoneware', *ECC Trans* Vol. 2 No. 6, 1939

Rhoda Edwards, *Catalogue of Stoneware Pottery including the Woolley Collection,* Minet Library, Lambeth, 1973

Rhoda Edwards, *London Potters circa 1570-1710,* Journal of Ceramic History No. 6, Stoke-on-Trent, 1974

Roy Edwards, 'An Early 18th Century Waste Deposit from the Vauxhall Pottery', *ECC Trans.* Vol. 12, Pt. 1, 1984

G. A. Godden, *An illustrated Encyclopedia of British Pottery & Porcelain,* London, 1966

G. A. Godden, *British Pottery,* London, 1974

Dennis Haselgrove & John Murray, *John Dwight's Fulham Pottery 1672-1978,* Journal of Ceramic History No. 11, Stoke-on-Trent, 1979.

W. B. Honey, 'English Saltglazed Stoneware', *ECC Trans.* No. 1, 1933

John Howell, 'The East Anglian Gotch', *ECC Trans.* Vol. 10, pt. 3, 1978

Reg & Philomena Jackson and Roger Price, *Bristol Potters and Potteries 1600-1800,* Journal of Ceramic History No. 12, Stoke-on-Trent, 1982

Esmé Lloyd, 'The Country Potteries of St. Helens and Prescot', *NCS Newsletter* No. 45, March 1982

Arnold Mountford, *The Illustrated Guide to Staffordshire Salt-Glazed Stoneware,* London, 1971

R. Myer, *Chats on Old English Tobacco Jars,* London 1930

Adrain Oswald and R. G. Hughes, 'Nottingham & Derbyshire Stoneware', *ECC Trans.* Vol. 9, Pt. 2, 1974

Adrian Oswald, R. J. C. Hildyard, R. G. Hughes, *English Brown Stoneware,* London 1982

Sylvia Pryor & Kevin Blockley, 'A 17th Century Kiln Site at Woolwich', *Post-Med. Arch.* Vol. 12, 1978

A. Parker, 'A Nottingham Pottery', *Trans. Thoroton Society,* Vol. XXXVI, 1933

W. J. Pountney, *Old Bristol Potteries,* Bristol, 1920

B. Rackham, & H. Read, *English Pottery,* London, 1924

B. Rackham, 'Dwight Figures: New Acquisitions at South Kensington', *Burlington Mag.* Vol. LVIII, 1931

B. Rackham, *Catalogue of the Glaisher Collection of Pottery & Porcelain in the Fitzwilliam Musuem Cambridge,* Cambridge, 1935

B. Rackham, 'A Dated Staffordshire Mug in the National Museum of Wales', *ECC Trans,* No. 8, Vol. 2, 1942

Alan Smith, *Illustrated Guide to Liverpool Herculaneum Pottery,* London, 1970

Hugh Tait, 'A Stoneware Election (?) Jug of 1705', *Antiquaries Journal* Vol. L, 1970

Richard Tyler, *Francis Place,* City Art Gallery, York, 1971

Richard Tyler, 'Francis Place's Pottery', *ECC Trans.* Vol. 8, Pt. 2, 1972

Graham Wilkinson, *A History of Local Potteries,* Bradford Art Galleries & Museums 1981

Pamela Wood, *Made at Nottm. A History of Saltglazed Stoneware,* Nottingham Castle Museum, 1980